HGV LAW GUIDE

HGV LAW GUIDE

DENNIS SUMMERS

BUTTERWORTHS
London Boston Sydney Wellington Durban Toronto

First published 1981

©Butterworth & Co (Publishers) Ltd, 1981

British Library Cataloguing in Publication Data

Summers, Dennis
  HGV law guide.
  1. Commercial vehicles – Law and legislation
  – Great Britain
  I. Title
  344.103′944   KD2625

  ISBN 0-408-00569-6 ✓

Photoset by Butterworths Litho Preparation Department
Printed in England by Billing & Sons Ltd.,
Guildford, London and Worcester

PREFACE

Through my experience as a road traffic Police Officer dealing with HGVs and their drivers, it has become increasingly obvious that the Regulations are not clear as they stand, but once explained in layman's terms this problem is easily overcome.

It is unfortunate that the driver should be so vulnerable when in fact his error is often made through ignorance or misunderstanding; whereas an endorsement to a driver is a serious occurrence, a £500 fine does not greatly hurt the average limited company.

This book is aimed at helping drivers, operators, driver/owners, road traffic Police and the like, to comprehend these Regulations by simplifying complexities of legislation.

The Regulations covered in these chapters are not always dealt with in sequence – numerical order is disturbed where the subject would be more clearly and comprehensively covered by doing so. Regulations not dealt with are those which are unimportant to HGV drivers and operators, and those which are well known or commonly understood.

In preparing this book I have consulted the Regulations directly and drawn upon my practical experience. I hope that the points made will benefit all those connected with working HGVs.

D.S.

CONTENTS

Chapter 1

THE MOTOR VEHICLES CONSTRUCTION AND USE REGULATIONS 1978

The *Motor Vehicles Construction and Use Regulations 1978*
cancelled out the last issue made in 1973 and brought together all
the vast number of amendments made during the intervening
period. They also include several new sub-paragraphs to existing
regulations, which affect commercial drivers and owners,
particularly in relation to tyres, plus a new definition – 'composite
trailers' – with conditions of its use, and an important piece which
has been added to the 'dangerous load' regulation. There are
many more.

Basically, these regulations are split into four parts:

Part 1 – *Definition*: Explains the meanings of certain expressions
used within the Regulations. Examples of these are such things as
what an 'exhaust brake' is, and explains fully; on the other end of
the scale it tells you what 'engineering plant' is. Although this may
sound all too technical, this definition part (particularly **Regulation
3**) answers quite a lot of commercial vehicle users' queries on
many aspects of construction.

Part 2 – *Construction*: This deals with the fitting of component
parts of vehicles, and weights, lengths, etc. of vehicles and trailers.
Generally, vehicles are constructed by reputable manufacturers
who comply with all the details of their construction. Often,
however, to adapt a vehicle for a certain purpose, e.g. to carry a
specific load such as hay or straw, a commercial user will alter a
vehicle by extending the bed, or chassis, and then fail to keep
within the maximum length allowable. This is just one example
where a user could quite innocently commit an offence by altering

or adapting a goods vehicle, whereas Part Two of the regulations may have given him the answer in the first place.

This Part also details the maximum widths permitted for all classes of vehicles and trailers, and includes what types of brakes etc. have to be fitted to these different classes. Again, this is of good use to someone perhaps making up his own trailer, but usually we can disregard such things because they are taken care of at manufacture stage.

Part 3 – *Use*: This part of the regulations is really the most important of all to the driver of a vehicle. It deals mainly with the maintenance of parts of the vehicle while it is being used on a road, and it is here where a driver is placed in a rather unusual – almost unfair – position.

Basically, many of the maintenance offences created by the *Construction and Use Regulations* carry driving licence endorsements, but a fleet operator formed into a limited company, which may be unfortunate enough to find it has committed an offence, will escape the endorsement because there is no individual licence holder, but a group of directors. However, the driver of their vehicle comes out of the incident with an endorsed licence. This affects the one-vehicle operator/driver in the same manner, unless he has formed a limited company, but this is not usual for the one-vehicle man.

Still, this situation has to be accepted, but it does point to the fact that the driver, in whose hands the fate of the vehicle rests most of the time, should at all times be on his guard.

In the following chapters most of the requirements of the Regulations, especially where they affect the commercial driver, will be condensed into simple form together with, where needed, some useful tips on traffic regulations in general.

Part 4 – *Schedules*: No offences are created by the Schedules but they do explain in complete detail additional requirements in respect of some of the regulations.

For example, **Regulations 139** and **140** deal with the carrying of wide and long loads and require operators to comply with certain conditions if these loads exceed certain dimensions. The regulation creates the offence and the schedule lays down the conditions with which to comply before moving the load. So, if an abnormally long or wide load is moved and the schedule conditions are not complied with, then the operator commits an offence of moving a load which exceeds the normal dimensions – he does not commit an offence of failing to notify Police etc.

To sum up then, the *Construction and Use Regulations* wrap up in a tidy but complicated bundle all that is required, with general classes of vehicles and trailers in respect of their manufacture, maintenance and use on the roads.

The manufacturer plays his part to a very high degree, and the maintenance of commercial vehicles in use is watched upon somewhat by means of the annual test, but the responsibility for making sure his vehicle is always roadworthy and safe is placed right in the lap of the professional driver, and it is with this last point in mind that this book has been written.

NOTES ON DEFINITIONS

Some definitions relating to vehicles and component parts not only make interesting reading, they are also very important.

One of these, in my experience so subtle, has caused more confusion than any other, yet in several regulaions the difference between terms has been vital. When one looks at the definitions of 'motor vehicle' and 'vehicle', the point I am making about confusion will be obvious.

In several regulations the word 'vehicle' appears, and many people, including those who are engaged in many aspects of transport, will interpret this term as meaning 'motor vehicle'. Well, a motor vehicle is a 'mechanically-propelled vehicle' – and that doesn't include a trailer. However, a vehicle seems to be any device running on wheels other than a motor vehicle, e.g. a trailer. This point emphasises the importance of reading every part of all traffic legislation very carefully.

Articulated vehicle

There are many different slants on the definition of this type of vehicle. It is generally known that for the speed limit regulations, however the vehicle is made up, whether the tractor is running separate or with its trailer, then it is always classed as an 'articulated vehicle'.

Some arguments say that it's one vehicle, some say it's two. But the *Road Traffic Act* says that it is 'a vehicle that can be divided into two parts both of which are vehicles'.

The *Construction and Use Regulations* travel right in those footsteps by defining it as 'a heavy motor-car with a trailer attached to the drawing vehicle .....', but if no part of the trailer is superimposed then it's not an articulated vehicle.

Hybrid vehicle

Although this term is not widely used, nor liked by many authorities for that matter, hybrid vehicles do exist. Vehicles used are classified in one way or another according to their construction or adaptation.

The important example for HGVs is the cab and chassis being driven to a body builder. If it is simply a power unit, cab, wheels and chassis then it is not a 'motor vehicle'. It fits no classification under any traffic acts and becomes a hybrid, and is exempted from many if not all regulations.

Close-coupled

This means that the wheels on two axles of a trailer and on the same side, do not exceed 1 m measured between the centre points of both axles.

Dual-purpose vehicle

Although not falling within any HGV classification, this is a definition often sought but not always at hand.

If a vehicle:
    (a) Is under 2040 kg (unladen),
    (b) Is constructed to carry both goods and passengers, and
    (c) Its drive is, or can be, transmitted to all of its wheels,
       then it is a dual-purpose vehicle.

Or, if a vehicle:
    (a) Is under 2040 kg (unladen),
    (b) Is constructed to carry both goods and passengers,
    (c) Has at least two proper seats fitted transversely to the rear of the driver,
    (d) Has glass each side of at least 1850 sq. cm area, and at the rear of at least 770 sq. cm area,
    (e) Has more than one row of seats in rear, with the distance between the steering wheel and the back of the last row of seats being not less than ⅓ of the distance between the steering wheel and the rear of the floor of the vehicle,
       then it is also a dual-purpose vehicle.

Rigid vehicle

This term is applied to a motor vehicle which is neither constructed nor adapted to form part of an articulated vehicle.

Brake drum

For the purposes of the *Construction and Use Regulations* a brake drum is *part of the wheel* and *not* part of the braking system.

Wheels

Except for the purpose of **Regulation 108 (Tyres)** of the *Construction and Use Regulations*, any two wheels of a motor vehicle or trailer shall be regarded as one wheel if the distance between the two contact centres is less than 460 mm.

Axles

Except for the purpose of **Regulation 108 (Tyres)** of the *Construction and Use Regulations*, any axle combination shall be regarded as one axle if the distance between any pair of axle centres is less than 1.02 m.

Hobo axles: In most respects, especially in the testing regulations and tyre regulations, overhang hobo axles are counted as running axles.

Type approval

This phrase is used in certain regulations within the *Construction and Use Regulations*, and it simply refers to a certificate issued in the UK by the Secretary of State, or his equivalent in other EEC member countries.

It approves the use of some components in vehicles at manufacture state, and it is issued to the vehicle manufacturer.

The introduction of Type Approval Certificates was instigated as a result of the forming of the European Community, and really the objective was the standardisation of certain safety aspects of vehicles to ensure that parts conformed to the same standard. Included are door locks, protective steering mechanism, exhaust gas and air pollution, and so on.

Bearing in mind the previous comments about the *Construction and Use Regulations 1978*, and explanations in respect of the making of such regulations, what follows is really what effects parts of the regulations, without the fancy words, could have on the commercial user and owner/driver.

To start with, here are some definitions which, although they are from the *Road Traffic Act 1972*, are important and possibly will need to be referred to at times during our progress through the regulations:

(a) *Heavy locomotive*: Vehicle not constructed to carry a load (other than tools, etc.): weight unladen exceeding 11 684 kg.
(b) *Light locomotive*: Vehicle not constructed to carry a load (other than tools, etc.): weight unladen exceeding 7366 kg but not exceeding 11 684 kg.
(c) *Motor tractor*: Vehicle not constructed to carry a load (other than tools, etc.): weight unladen not exceeding 7366 kg.
(d) *Motor car*: Vehicle constructed to carry (i) passengers, or (ii) a load:
  If (i) *passengers*: to carry not more than seven persons and effects: not to exceed 3048 kg unladen.
  If (ii) *a load*: to carry goods of any description: not to exceed 3048 kg unladen.
  Any vehicle not falling in either (i) or (ii): not to exceed 2540 kg unladen.
(e) *Heavy motor car*: vehicle, not being a motor car, constructed to carry a load or passengers: weight unladen exceeding 2540 kg.

Remember, artic users, that for this purpose 'vehicle' means the unit and trailer together; more importantly, if the unit is being used without the semi it is still classed as 'a goods-carrying vehicle'.

We will, perhaps, jump from regulation to regulation, but only so that those dealing with lengths, widths, etc., can be kept together though under separate headings.

REGULATION 3

Overhang (of vehicle, not load)

Completely confuses one in explaining how overhang of the bed of the vehicle, beyond the rearmost axle, is measured. So beware if you intend to extend rearwards.

Generally then – (in *Figure 1*) distance B must not exceed distance A by more than 60%. One exception to this is a tipper – this can exceed 60% by 1.15 m.

LENGTHS

Regulations 9, 73 and **136** following deal with maximum vehicle lengths, including those for trailers and combinations.

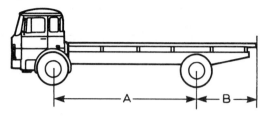

Figure 1 Rear overhang limit

REGULATION 9

Artics

Must not exceed 15 m (but if normally used for the carriage of indivisible long loads, can extend to 18.3 m).

Rigids

Must not exceed 11 m.

REGULATION 73 – TRAILERS

Generally, two-wheeled trailers must not exceed 7 m, but this can be extended to 12 m if it has not less than four wheels and is drawn by a vehicle the unladen weight of which exceeds 2030 kg.

Exemptions: Indivisible-load trailer carrying long loads,
Articulated trailer,
Broken-down vehicle being towed, and
Trailer used for repair of roads (road razer, etc.).

REGULATION 136 – COMBINATIONS

Lengths

Locomotive: Can draw up to three trailers.
Motor tractor: Can draw one laden, two unladen.
Heavy motor car/motor car: Can draw one.

A vehicle towing *one* trailer – *not* to exceed 18 m in total length. (If the trailer is normally used to carry loads of exceptional length, or in the case of a broken-down vehicle being towed, then the 18 m rule does not apply.)

A vehicle towing *two or more* trailers – *only one* can exceed 7 m long.

A vehicle drawing *three* trailers – *no* trailer in the combination is to exceed 7 m.

Remember: If you intend using push-pull methods in combination then both the push and pull vehicles must be included in the above measurements, and these combinations are to be measured from the leading point of the front vehicle to the trailing point of the rear vehicle.

Widths

The maximum widths of all commercial vehicles are controlled under several separate regulations, and *remember*, this is width from outside edge to outside edge of the vehicle, not the width of the load.

It is simplest just to put out the widths under headings, as follows:

Locomotives:	Regulation 48 – 2.75 m
Motor tractors:	Regulation 53 – 2.5 m
Heavy motor cars:	Regulation 57 – 2.5 m
Motor cars:	Regulation 62 – 2.5 m
Trailers:	Regulation 74 – 2.3 m

For trailers, the limit of 2.3 m shown above can be extended to 2.5 m if the trailer is being drawn by a locomotive, motor tractor or heavy motor car, or where it forms part of an artic, but in these cases the towing unit *must exceed* 2030 kg and the width of the trailer must not extend beyond the width of the towing unit on each side by more than 305 mm.

Remember: Do not let these widths mix you up with maximum widths of vehicles running under the *Special Types Order 1973*.

HEIGHTS

Maximum heights of vehicles only ever applied to public service vehicles, and for these it is 4.57 m. But **Regulation 80A** now requires (since 6 March 1979) that if the heights of the vehicles listed below extend to over 12′, then a plate indicating maximum height must be fitted to the cab where it will be in full view of the driver when he is in his driving position:

(a) Vehicles capable of hoisting and carrying skips,
(b) Vehicles carrying containers (includes container-carrying trailers and semi-trailers), and
(c) Vehicles which are engineering plant, or carrying engineering equipment (includes trailers and semi-trailers carrying engineering equipment).

REGULATION 11

This deals with compensating wheels on commercial vehicles, and it says that vehicles and trailers with more than four wheels, and semi-trailers with more than two wheels, must be fitted with compensating gear, so that *all* the wheels will stay in contact with the road.

The regulation doesn't apply to any steerable wheel of a motor vehicle if the load on the wheel does not exceed 3560 kg.

REGULATION 12

We all know that motor vehicles and trailers have to be fitted with a spring between each wheel and the chassis – this regulation directs so – but there are vehicles which surprisingly don't need springs!

(a) Trailers used for hauling felled timber,
(b) Road-sweeping vehicles, and
(c) Vehicles under 4070 kg and used mainly for road-making and travelling over rough ground.

REGULATION 17

This deals with seat belts and anchorage points, but the *only* goods vehicles that require these to be fitted are those manufactured after 1 September 1966, registered on or after 1 April 1967, and having an unladen weight not exceeding 1525 kg.

But, under **Regulation 17A**, goods vehicles first used after 1 April 1980 and having a plated gross weight of up to 3500 kg, and passenger vehicles with up to 12 seats, have to be fitted with seat belts for the driver and specified front passenger's seat.

REGULATION 18

All goods-carrying vehicles must be fitted with a speedometer to indicate the vehicle's speed, and this must be readily visible to the driver at all times.

Remember: Although the speedo is allowed a 10% margin of error in recording, if it is 10% out of accurate this doesn't give you 10% over on speed limits!

REGULATION 98

Requires you to keep your speedo in good working order. However, don't worry too much if the drive cable breaks or the indicating hand breaks off; you don't commit any offence if the fault occurred on the journey or if steps have been taken to rectify the defect, i.e. new part ordered or vehicle booked in for defect to be put right.

REGULATION 19

All petrol-driven motor vehicles used on or after 1 July 1973 must have a metal fuel tank, and this includes any tank containing fuel used to drive equipment or plant which is part of the vehicle.

REGULATION 104

This requires that the petrol tank be properly maintained.

REGULATIONS 23, 24

At least two mirrors have to be fitted to all goods vehicles to assist the driver to be aware of traffic to the rear and to both sides rearwards of the vehicle.

That means that you must have *one offside externally* and *one nearside externally* on all vehicles, including small goods vehicles and transit-style vehicles. The belief that the external nearside one can be left off if an internal one is fitted no longer applies.

Remember: Mirrors must be fitted in such a way that they remain steady under driving conditions.

Also, external mirrors must be visible to the driver from his driving position through either a side window or that part of the windscreen swept by the wiper blade.

Every exterior mirror fitted to the driver's side of the vehicle (unless it's a spring-back) has to be capable of being adjusted by the driver when he is in his driving position. But, this does not prevent the driver from adjusting the mirror from outside the vehicle provided that it can be locked into that position.

REGULATIONS 27, 28

One *or more* automatic wipers must be fitted to the windscreen, and these must be capable of clearing the windscreen so that the driver can clealy see the road in front of both the *nearside* and *offside* of the vehicle.

A washer must be fitted in conjunction with each wiper so that the areas swept by the wipers are clear of mud and similar deposits.

Remember: This requirement applies to all times – wet or shine – and both wipers and washers must be fully working as well.

REGULATION 29

A horn *that works* has to be fitted to every HGV, and if it was fitted after 1 August 1973 its note must be *continuous* – so no Col. Bogeys, twin tones, sirens, or bells! It seems that ships' fog-horns are acceptable.

REGULATIONS 30, 106

Generally, HGVs have to be fitted with a 'suitable contrivance' to reduce the noise caused by the exhaust gas escaping – these are always fitted by the manufacturer, but once fitted they have to be maintained. We commonly call them 'silencers', and these regulations require that:

(a) A silencer must be fitted,
(b) It must not be altered in any way to increase noise,
(c) It must be in good condition, i.e. not rusted through, and
(d) Exhaust gas must not escape at the manifold or front pipe – it must pass through the silencer.

REGULATIONS 33, 34, 109, 110, 111, 112

Although smoke emission through excess fuel use by cold-start devices and the like on both petrol and diesel engines are covered by what are known as the 'smoke regulations' (they are all coupled to the same offence), and how much black soot is being blown out of the tail-pipe!

The Department of Transport usually deals with this problem as a delayed prohibition, and the Police use a similar method of caution to allow the operator to complete his journey until workshop treatment is available.

There is a bit of a sting in the tail of this set of regulations – this deals with other things that find themselves being emitted from motor vehicle engines – grit, sparks and ashes, for example! One other important present-day substance which is mentioned is oil. If oil dripping from a vehicle causes damage to a person or property, then an offence is committed.

Good maintenance is such an essential part of prevention in what must be, apart from speeding, one of the most common offences.

Remember: Continued spewing out of smoke rearwards can cover light clusters and index plates with soot – this can be a serious offence and would perhaps carry a severe penalty.

REGULATIONS 41, 105

At first these seem to be complicated regulations – 41 requires motor vehicles to be fitted with lamps while 105 requires the lamps to be properly maintained and clean.

These regulations deal with motor vehicles only *not* trailers and their use during the hours of daylight, *not* darkness. If lamps are fitted to the vehicle then they must be fitted so as to render the vehicle capable of being driven safely during the hours of darkness – which means that:

(a) No lights, front or rear, need be fitted to a motor vehicle being used during daylight hours (unless in fog or heavy rain, etc.).

(b) If lights are fitted there must be two white lights to the front and two red lights to the rear, plus two red reflectors to the rear. *And these must be maintained during daylight hours.*

Remember: Trailers require tail lamps only during the hours of darkness, but they may require stop lamps and indicators *at all times.*

Note: Stop lamps and direction indicators for *all* vehicles and trailers are dealt with under the *Road Vehicles (Lighting) Regulations 1971*.

Likewise, all other aspects of lighting are dealt with by other legislation, and these will have to be referred to. Generally, they are:

(a) Position and height/inboard measurements, etc.: *Road Traffic Act 1972* and *Road Vehicles (Lighting) Regulations 1971*.
(b) Spot/fog/search/orange beacons, etc.: *Road Vehicles (Lighting) Regulations 1971*.
(c) Rear number plate illumination: *Excise Act 1971*.
(d) Reversing lights: *Road Vehicles (Lighting) Regulations 1971*.

Remember: Any lamp showing to the front over 7 watts strength is a headlamp. Be careful when fitting that extra 'handy' lamp, such as a swivel lamp – it could be an illegal headlamp.

To sum up – all lighting regulations are vast and complicated. The *Construction and Use Regulations* requires only that lights be fitted to the front and rear of the vehicle, and that these lights should be maintained *during daylight hours*.

REGULATION 42

Most HGVs are required to be plated and tested on their first anniversary by the Department of Transport, and each year thereafter.

Generally, if the vehicle is load-carrying and its tare weight exceeds 1525 kg, it must be plated and tested under the *Goods Vehicle (Plating and Testing) Regulations 1971*.

But HGVs, during the first year of operation, must comply with the details of the manufacturer's plate to which this regulation refers; likewise, trailers over 1020 kg tare weight. This plate, usually fixed on the nearside of the vehicle or trailer, gives the maximum gross and axle weights to be transmitted to the road surface.

That is straightforward enough, but what happens to goods vehicles which do not exceed 1525 kg? They simply have to be tested annually the same as a private car, but if used on or after 1 January 1968 then a manufacturer's plate *restricting the gross and axle weights* is fitted and this had to be complied with during the working life of the vehicle.

Remember: This type of goods vehicle used before 1 January 1968 has no plating weight restrictions at all, but overloading of this vehicle may produce an offence within another regulation, i.e. 'dangerous load' or using a vehicle for a purpose other than for which it was intended.

Load-carrying trailers of under 1020 kg *first* used before 1 January 1968 do not require plating at all. Similarly, trailers *first* used on and after 1 January 1968 do not require plating. But *all* vehicles (including private cars) and *all* load-carrying trailers, of whatever tare weight, *first* used after 1 October 1981 must be plated by the manufacturer, restricting its gross and axle weights.

Small goods-vehicle operators who intend towing trailers – beware!

REGULATIONS 47 TO 79

These deal specifically with maximum widths, the required number of wheels or axles to be equipped with brakes, types of tyres to be fitted and which wheels require wings.

One must remember that as far as the *motor vehicles* under all the headings are concerned, the manufacturer is required to comply with these specific items when building the vehicle.

What does sometimes cause problems is when an operator extends the bed of a vehicle for a short distance on each side, albeit to support an extra piece of a load.

Remember: If you do extend the bed of a vehicle then it comes within the definition of the width of the vehicle, and generally no HGV shall exceed 2.5 m overall.

The only complications which seem to occur many times within these regulations are those dealing with trailers. Presumably this is because some operators either make up their own trailers, or specify to a builder so that they have a trailer which can do a specific operation.

REGULATIONS 73 – TRAILERS

Length

Load-carrying trailers with up to two wheels must not exceed 7 m, but this length can be extended to 12 m for a trailer with four or more wheels. If the length is increased to this maximum then:

Remember: The towing unit must have a tare weight of at least 2030 kg and A (*Figure 2*) must not be less than ⅗ of the total trailer length, B.

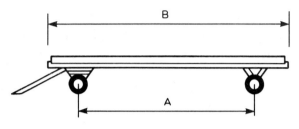

Figure 2 Trailer length proportions

Note: In measuring the maximum trailer length the tow bar does not have to be included. Exceptions to the above are:

(a) Abnormal load trailers (see Chapter 2),
(b) Articulated trailers (see **Regulation 9**),
(c) Broken-down vehicle towing, and
(d) Most trailers used for road repairs.

In these cases lengths *can* be increased *up to* 18.3 m.

REGULATION 74 – TRAILERS

Widths

Load-carrying trailers must not exceed 2.3 m in width, generally, but this can be increased to 2.5 m in the following cases:

(a) If the trailer is towed by a heavy motor car, or
(b) If the trailer is part of an articulated outfit, but in this case the unit tare weight must exceed 2030 kg.

REGULATION 75 – TRAILERS

Brakes

Every load-carrying trailer the weight of which exceeds 102 kg must be fitted with an efficient braking system.

Let us clear up over-run braking systems first.

(a) If the trailer was manufactured before 27 February 1977 then the laden weight must not exceed 3560 kg.

(b) If it was manufactured on or after 27 February 1977 then the laden weight must not exceed 3500 kg.

That is as far as one can go and get away with over-run brakes.

Most trailers used by HGV operators will not fall within the scope of the over-run system and in that case an electric, air pressure, or similar system is fitted.

But in either case the following are guiding factors:

(a) Trailers manufactured before 1 January 1968 must have the braking system operating on at least two wheels if the trailer has not more than four wheels, and on at least four wheels if the trailer has more than four wheels.

In this case the brakes can be applied from the towing unit by the driver (by pressing the footbrake or operating some other device), or by some other person on the towing unit or the trailer (by operating a lever or similar device).

(b) Trailers manufactured on or after 1 January 1968 must have a braking system which operates on all wheels of the trailer, and is capable of being applied by the driver using the same means of operation as when applying the brakes of the towing unit.

Also, in case there is failure of any part of the braking system on the towing unit or the trailer, there must be a secondary system to operate the trailer brakes.

All trailers must have an efficient *mechanical* parking brake, generally capable of holding the trailer on a gradient of at least 1:6.25.

REGULATION 76 – TRAILERS

Wings

Wings have to be fitted to the rear wheels of trailers with more than two wheels, but in the case of two-wheeled trailers to both wheels.

If the body protects the wheels, as shown in *Figure 3*, then wings are not required. Some HGV-type vehicles, as follows, are exempt from having wings fitted:

(a) Trailers used for carriage of round timber only (whether laden or unladen).

(b) Trailers in unfinished condition (to works for completion only).

(c) Vehicle being towed as a result of breakdown.

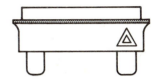

Figure 3 Trailer wings not required

REGULATION 80

All HGVs with a tare weight in excess of 2540 kg must have the tare weight of the vehicle painted on the nearside.

REGULATION 81 – TRAILER PLATE

Unless the trailer is:

(a) An articulated trailer together with towing unit,

(b) Broken-down vehicle,

(c) Trailer for round timber, or

(d) The trailer is fitted with reflectors as required by the *Motor Vehicles (Lighting) Regulations 1971*, then a plate must be fitted to the rear of the trailer or, where more than one trailer is towed, to the rearmost trailer. Shape and measurements as in *Figure 4* apply.

Important: Trailers alone are allowed to carry *triangular-shaped reflectors*; in fact this is the only shape that trailers can carry, and it must have a white background 12 mm wide.

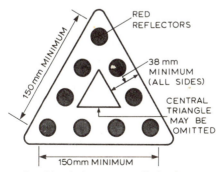

Figure 4 Trailer rear plate. Must be in centre or offside of centre, and base no higher than 1.4 m from the ground

Remember: Reflectors other than those mentioned above, including side reflectors and vehicle reflectors, other than trailer plates, are provided for in the *Motor Vehicles (Lighting) Regulations 1971*.

REGULATIONS 85 TO 92 (EXCEPT 87), SCHEDULES 6, 7

Permissible maximum weights of rigids, articulated vehicles and tow-bar trailers

These regulations refer to every type and combination of HGV and their use in relation to the maximum amount of gross weight, single-axle weight and combination of axle weights, that can be transmitted to the road surface by that vehicle or combination of vehicles.

However one is involved with HGVs, it will be generally agreed that this is a complicated set of regulations that few fully understand. All sorts of red herrings appear in each regulation, including what types of braking systems are fitted and whether plates are fitted by the Department of Transport or the manufacturer, and so on.

If one adds to this vehicles separated by two, three, four, five or six axles, tranverse wheels, and axle combinations, then the reader can quickly see that chapters rather than pages could be written on the subject.

Firstly, let's dispense with rigid vehicles because they are plated by either the manufacturer or the Department of Transport to restrict gross and axle weights. Perhaps just as important is the fact that it is not practice for the distance betwen the axles of a rigid vehicle ever to vary.

Likewise with draw-bar trailers, which also are plated by either the Department of Transport or the manufacturer, their axle spacings never vary. Therefore, one simply complies with the plate as guidance to maximum weights to be carried.

Articulated tractor units really come under the same heading of permissible maximum weights and if a unit is *always* used with the *same* semi-trailer, or on its own, then it falls into the same category.

So, in breaking down what are apparently extremely difficult regulations, concern arises only when an operator has to mismatch tractors and trailers as articulated combinations. These facts are just as important for the driver who is regularly sent to hook up to a variety of trailers, because when he varies the axle spacings the plated weights of the unit alter and have to comply with weights in relation to axle spacings.

Figures 5 to *8* show the maximum permitted weights as applicable to articulated outfits and their axle spread.

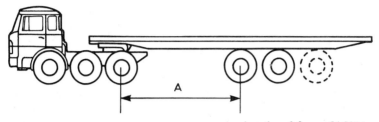

Figure 5 Axle spacings – maximum train weights. Two- or three-axle trailer with three-axle tractor unit

A – less than 2.0 m – 24 390 kg
at least 2.0   – 26 420
"   2.3   – 28 450
"   3.2   – 30 490
"   4.0   – 32 520

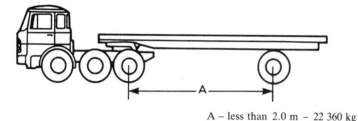

Figure 6 Axle spacings – maximum train weights. Single-axle trailer with three-axle tractor unit

A – less than 2.0 m – 22 360 kg
at least 2.0   – 24 390
"   2.7   – 26 420
"   3.0   – 28 450
"   4.0   – 30 490
"   4.4   – 32 520

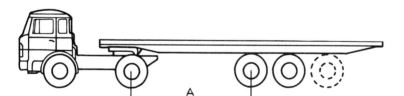

Figure 7 Axle spacings – maximum train weights. Two- or three-axle trailer with two-axle tractor unit

A – less than 2.9 m – 24 390 kg
at least 2.9   – 26 420
"   3.1   – 28 450
"   3.6   – 30 490
"   4.2   – 32 520

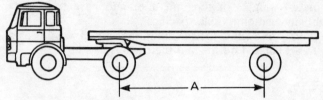

Figure 8 Axle spacings – maximum train
weights. Single-axle trailer with two-axle
tractor unit

A – less than 2.1 m – 20 330 kg
at least 2.1 – 22 360
        ”   3.1 – 24 390

The maximum imposed weight on a two-wheeled axle is: **9150 kg**
If fitted with twin wheels with a minimum of 300 mm tyre centres,
or with single wide tyres, the maximum is: **10 170 kg**
For axles of the twin oscillating type (four in line) the maximum is:
                                                        11 180 kg
However, the high limit of 11 180 kg does not apply if the axle
forms part of a two-axled or three-axled bogie, as defined in
Regulation 92 as 'closely-spaced', that is:

Two-axled bogie: Having axles not more than 2.5 m and not less
than 1.02 m apart.

Three-axled bogie: Having the outermost axles not more than
3.25 m apart and no one axle has a plated weight exceeding
7630 kg.

Maximum bogie weights

Closely-spaced – two-axled: This is applicable, in each case, if
each axle has equal plated weights (*Figure 9*).

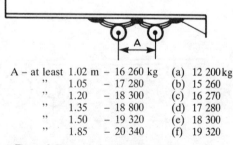

A – at least 1.02 m – 16 260 kg   (a) 12 200 kg
        ”   1.05   – 17 280   (b) 15 260
        ”   1.20   – 18 300   (c) 16 270
        ”   1.35   – 18 800   (d) 17 280
        ”   1.50   – 19 320   (e) 18 300
        ”   1.85   – 20 340   (f) 19 320

Figure 9 Two-axle bogie weight limits

If each axle in a two-axled bogie has unequal plated weights the
maximum axle weights in (a) to (f) *Figure 9* are applicable.

Closely-spaced – three-axled (Figure 10).
Note: See definition of 'closely-spaced' previously.

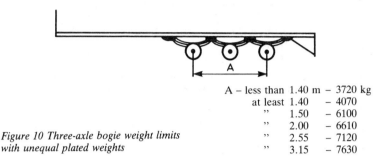

A – less than	1.40 m	–	3720 kg
at least	1.40	–	4070
"	1.50	–	6100
"	2.00	–	6610
"	2.55	–	7120
"	3.15	–	7630

*Figure 10 Three-axle bogie weight limits
with unequal plated weights*

Three-axled bogies: Where plated weight of any axle exceeds 7630 kg (*Figure 11*).

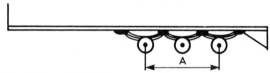

A – less than 3.0 m – 18 290 kg
    at least 3.0 m and centre axle plated not more than 8390 kg – 20 330 kg
      ,,   3.8 m and centre axle plated not more than 8640 kg – 22 360 kg
      ,,   4.6 m and centre axle plated not more than 9150 kg – 24 390 kg

*Figure 11 Three-axle bogie weight limits where plated weight
of any axle exceeds 7630 kg*

REGULATION 87

Perhaps the final word is with draw-bar trailers whilst being towed by rigids. Remember that these are plated and, as already mentioned, axle spacings will rarely vary.
    Combinations in these circumstances fall into two categories:
  (i) A maximum of 24 390 kg.
  (ii) If the trailer is fitted with power-assisted brakes which operate when the towing unit motor is stopped, and the driver has a brake warning pressure device, then the maximum is 32 520 kg.

REGULATION 97

This must be the regulation that creates more offences than any other in any part of traffic legislation.

For the authorities it is also a 'saver' regulation because it seems that in every vehicle 'stop and check' situation on the roadside invariably an offence can be found which fits this regulation.

The regulation is in three parts, and it would be almost impossible to enumerate the offences that could be committed under any one particular part, because they are so vast. All that is possible is to take each part separately and comment upon it, and then list a variety of incidents which have been held to be offences, and **remember**, the regulation applies to every motor vehicle *and* trailer.

Part 1 deals with:

    (a) All parts and accessories.
    (b) The number of passengers and the manner in which they are carried.
    (c) The weight, distribution, packing and adjustment of a load on a vehicle must be such that no danger is caused, *or is likely* to be caused, to any person on the vehicle or on the road.

Some examples of offences under this part are:

    (i) *Parts*:   Four out of nine wheel nuts missing; a spring leaf broken.
       Accessories: A wheel trim spinning off; a fuel tank overspilling when the vehicle keels over on bends.
    (ii) An offence would be committed if, for example, a driver carried, say, five passengers in his cab space, or if he foolishly decided to allow passengers to be carried either on the bed of the vehicle or on top of the load.
    (iii) Weight carried in excess of the plated weight is a separate offence, but under this heading come vehicles which have been that badly loaded, with so much to the rear axle, that the vehicle's front wheels have been lifted from the road surface.
    (iv) In packing, especially round containers, an offence would be committed if barrels or drums were allowed to roll around within the load-carrying part of the vehicle.

A rather unusual conviction under this heading occurred when a pantechnicon carried its load as shown in *Figure 12*. It was held that this was likely to cause danger because part of the load was borne by the tailboard – had it not been resting there but just protruding then perhaps there would have been no offence under this regulation.

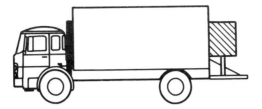

Figure 12 Load extending onto tailboard

A possible offence under this regulation, which perhaps is worth mentioning although no hard-and-fast decision was made, involved an articulated vehicle carrying a swimming pool, as shown in *Figure 13*. The driver and firm were prosecuted for 'no mirrors'. The firm appealed and the Lord Chief Justice allowed the appeal but commented that 'no offence was committed under the mirror regulations, but maybe an offence would have been committed under another regulation'.

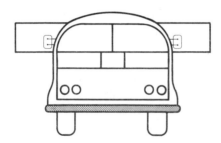

Figure 13 An overhanging load obscuring mirror rear view

Part 2: Again, this part applies to both motor vehicles and trailers, but deals particularly with the load carried and how it is secured.

In breaking down this part into reasonable understanding it is better to take it by stages.

A load has to be secured to the vehicle so that neither *danger* nor *nuisance* is *likely* to be caused to any person or to property. To prevent a load from either falling or being blown from the vehicle, it has to be secured properly.

So basically, if the load or part of the load is already on the road, it is an offence. If ropes have let go or broken and the load has shifted, it is an offence. Where dusty loads such as sand are carried, it has to be sheeted to prevent it from being blown about – otherwise, again it is an offence.

The degree of danger or nuisance caused may be a guiding factor as to a prosecution, but make no mistake – if a tomato being carried in a box on a vehicle rolls out onto the road, then an offence is complete.

Part 3: This also applies to both motor vehicles and trailers, and deals with vehicles which are used for a purpose other than which they are intended. Before giving an example of an offence one must be reminded that *danger* or *nuisance* to any persons should not be *likely* to be caused, whether they are on the vehicle or on the road.

The possibilities are numerous, but *Figure 14* shows one such use. It will be seen here that the trailer could move within the tow-bar free play, and move the load against the direction of the towing unit, thus being *likely* to cause danger.

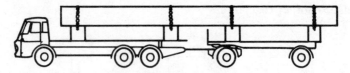

Figure 14 Vehicle and trailer used for purpose not intended

One must pause again to mention the vast scope of this regulation – it almost makes up for every loop-hole that other regulations have failed to cover. Beware – stated cases have been frequent over the years – chapters of discussion could easily be written – there are numerous stated cases yet to come I fear.

REGULATION 101 – MAINTENANCE OF BRAKES

Brakes are component parts of motor vehicles, and in this day and age, whatever we find ourselves driving, it is accepted that when applied, they will slow or stop the vehicle if the middle pedal of three is applied at the correct moment.

It is also a fact that, during the annual test or at roadside checks, an amazing number of HGVs are found to have braking defects which put them off the road!

This regulation, although appearing at a glance to be very short in actual text, requires one to comply with many aspects of a vehicle braking system. It deals with *every* part of *every* braking system of the vehicle and trailer, including the means of operation of the brakes, whether it be by foot pedals, levers, switches, or automatic devices.

All of these, while the vehicle or trailer is *being used on a road*, must be kept in good, efficient, working order and be properly adjusted.

These details apply only to the brakes which are required by legislation to be fitted to a vehicle. In other words, there are no regulations requiring electric retarders to be fitted, but many vehicles have them installed. If a defect develops in a retarder while the vehicle is on the road then no offence is created under this 'defective brakes' regulation.

The percentage of braking efficiency is another aspect of the regulation, but first it is best to mention a few facts about defective brakes.

If we can assume that every part of a system is fitted to the vehicle and, for example, a fault such as a line leak occurs and allows tank pressure to fall, then this would be an offence under this regulation.

On the other hand if, for example, a link piece of the braking system fell off the vehicle, thereby rendering the braking system useless, then since not all parts of the system are fitted to the vehicle this would become an offence of no brakes and not defective brakes.

Minimum braking efficiencies are subject to the same regulation but of course are an entirely different aspect. Efficiencies can be tested only by special equipment.

Again, the regulations complicate these requirements and to make things as clear as possible the following may assist in arriving at vehicle braking efficiencies which are the minimum required.

Before this, however, it is important to understand the difference between a post-1968 and pre-1968 vehicle, because it will be found that efficiencies for the two types of vehicles differ.

A pre-October 1968 vehicle: refers to rigids only. No manufacturers plate was required to be fitted, therefore the vehicle was restricted to 14 224 kg.

A prior-October 1968 vehicle: again, refers to rigids only, but it was fitted with a manufacturer's plate, and dependent on axle spread, increased its gross maximum weight to either 15 240 kg or 16 256 kg.

A post-October 1968 vehicle: all these vehicles had to be fitted with manufacturers' plates.

Please refer to these definitions in relation to the following list of required percentage efficiencies.

(a) **Pre-1968 two-axled – rigids:**
Service 45%   Secondary 20%
(b) **Pre-1968 multi-axled – rigids and articulated vehicles:**
Service 40%   Secondary 15%
(c) **Prior- and post-1968 – all types:**
Service 50%   Secondary 25%   Parking 16%
The only exceptions to the requirements of (c) are *artic tractors* with *secondary* on the front axle only – 20%
(d) **Semi-trailers:**
Manufactured before 1968 – plated *under* 6100 kg per axle
Service 32%
Manufactured before 1968 – plated *over* 6100 kg per axle
Service 35%
Manufactured during or after 1968 – plated *any* axle weight
Service 40%
Be careful: If a pre-1968 semi-trailer is not carrying a manufacturer's plate, and is mis-matched with a unit, then the percentage required could vary.
Draw-bar trailers:
Manufactured before 1968
Service 40%
Manufactured after 1968
Service 50%
All trailers manufactured during or after 1968
Parking brake 16%
Remember: Trailers manufactured before 1968 did not require a percentage efficiency on their parking brakes.

REGULATIONS 107, 108 – CONDITION AND MAINTENANCE OF TYRES

It must be emphasised at the outset that basically we are discussing here tyres which relate to or are fitted to HGVs. With tyre requirements in relation to other vehicles this has always been a source of confusion.

In the first instance remember that three persons can commit an offence in respect of tyre defects:

(i) The driver of the vehicle,
(ii) The operator (who may not be the driver), and
(iii) In certain hire vehicles, the owner.

Before any offence is committed the tyre has to be a pneumatic tyre and fitted to the wheel of a motor vehicle or trailer.

There are many offences created under different headings and, **remember**, a *separate offence* is committed by *each* single tyre defect.

I will deal with each heading separately, as follows:

(a) Fitting an unsuitable tyre in relation to other tyres fitted, or in regard to how the vehicle is being used.
Examples: A low-ply tyre being fitted to a vehicle carrying a very heavy load, or a narrow-tread tyre being used together with three wide-treaded tyres.

(b) Running a tyre low on pressure. An extremely difficult offence to prove. No doubt one for which expert evidence would almost certainly have to be called, even down to proving the accuracy of the pressure gauge!

(c) A break or cut in excess of 25 mm measured on the outside of the tyre, in any direction of the section width. Must be deep enough to reach body cords.

(d) A lump or bulge in any part caused by separation or failure of its structure.

(e) The tyre has ply or cord structure exposed.

(f) At least 1 mm of tread must be present for at least ¾ of the breadth of the tyre tread and around the whole circumference.

Depth gauges, if they are used to measure, would have to be proved accurate. In other words, gauges are used only in extreme cases, and offences under this heading are usually assured when the tyre either is devoid of tread altogether or has only a visible and not measureable tread pattern.

Remember: The whole circumference of the tyre doesn't have to be bald for ¾ of its width – just on the smallest part of the circumference is enough to have committed an offence.

If a Denovo-type tyre is fitted and it is being used while deflated then (c), (d) and (e) above do not apply.

In using re-cut tyres the only proviso is that fabric of the tyre should not be cut or exposed in the process.

The above paragraphs do not apply either to a broken-down vehicle or to a vehicle on its journey to be broken up – *if in both cases the vehicle is being towed at less than 20 mph.*

To complete Regulation 107, which seems to cover every possible loophole, it adds that any tyre on a motor vehicle or trailer, while in use on the road, should be fit for the purpose to which it is being put, and free from any defect which *in any way* may cause damage to the road or danger to any person on the vehicle or using the road.

Regulation 108 deals with the mixture of cross- (diagonal-) ply and radial tyres, and in this respect HGVs differ somewhat from other vehicles because of the number of axles they run on. (Bias-belted types are classed as radials.)

It is interesting to note that, as far as annual tests are concerned, conditions have been relaxed in relation to vehicles with twin wheels.

Generally, these are the requirements in relation to mixing:

Two-axled rigids – single-wheeled

The same tyres are advised on all wheels. The only mixture permitted is:

Front: Cross-plies   *Rear*: Radials

Two-axled rigids – twin rear wheels

The regulations require the same as for single-wheeled rigids, but the Department of Transport on test will not fail the vehicle if:

Front: Radials   *Rear (both wheels)*: Cross-plies

Six-wheeled rigids or artics – twin steering wheels

Can have radials on both steering axles. If running thus can then have cross-plies on the rear, and if cross-plies are fitted to the steering axles then radials can be fitted to the rear ones.

Six-wheeled – single drive (6 × 2)

Can have radials on drive axle – no other mixture permitted.

Multi-axled – eight-wheelers

Either full set of radials or front and cross-plies on rear two. Cannot mix twinning of axles, and the front pair of axles must be alike, likewise the rear pair of axles.

Mixing of radials and cross-ply tyres

Notes to Regulation 108

It must be emphasised that the diagrams in *Figures 15* and *16* related to these notes may not in all respects comply with the letter of the requirements of this regulation.

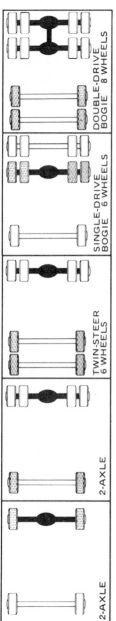

Figure 15 *Acceptable mixtures on rigids – radial/cross-ply tyres*

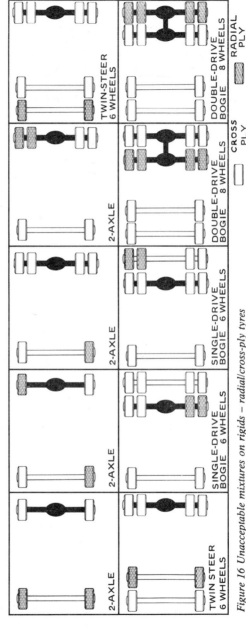

Figure 16 *Unacceptable mixtures on rigids – radial/cross-ply tyres*
NOTE: TRAILERS – DO NOT MIX ON THE SAME AXLE

However, it is accepted by the Department of Transport, in respect of annual tests, that certain mixtures are permissible on vehicles with twin wheels or multi-axles.

It would appear that in these circumstances it would become difficult for any authority to prosecute to the ultimate, provided that the vehicle had the relaxed type of mixtures.

Artic tractor units would, it appears, come under the same guide lines and be tested as to tyre mixtures in the same manner as rigids.

Trailers and semi-trailers are listed under the same requirements, i.e., that tyres are not to be mixed on the same axle.

Wide tyres

A wide tyre, as far as these regulations are concerned, is a tyre which has not less than 300 mm of its width in contact with the road surface.

If wide tyres are fitted on two-axled vehicles then mixing between radial-ply and cross-ply is permitted.

REGULATIONS 114, 115 – EXCESSIVE NOISE

Two distinct offences can be committed in relation to excessive noise.

(a) That noise which is caused by the vehicle itself while in use on a road, or
(b) The noise caused by the vehicle but only by reason that the driver is doing some action to cause the noise.

Perhaps a few examples of offences under each paragraph may give rise to discussion.

Under (a) (i) A tail-board not fixed properly and continually flapping.
(ii) Engine timing maladjustment causing erratic firing.

(The driver of the vehicle in respect of any offence in this regulation has a defence, provided that the noise was caused by a fault in design, or because there was negligence on the part of some other person who repaired or adjusted parts of the vehicle. Or, in the case of noise from the load of the vehicle, that person who packed or adjusted the load.)

Under (b) (i) Sounding the horn of the vehicle, perhaps to attract the attention of a colleague on the road.
(ii) Continually pressing the footbrake pedal to operate the release valve when it's not required.

Hard on the heels of regulations 114 and 115 come 116, 117 and 118 which are very closely related to offences by noise.

REGULATION 116 – NOISE METERS

Although a lot about noise meters is written into the regulations, and there is even a schedule seting out maximum sound levels, very few authorities use decibel meters for prosecutions.

The offence of *noise* is dealt with in so many other regulations that it's almost a case of taking a sledge hammer to crack a nut.

But the main reason that noise meters are not generally used is because most vehicles, in lost of respects, including noise, are what is known as 'type approved', and comply with the regulation when manufactured.

The Department of Transport may use noise meters if a vehicle, or several vehicles, are the subject of a complaint about the noise being caused.

REGULATION 117

Solely to prevent noise, this regulation requires the driver to switch off any machinery attached to or part of a motor vehicle when stationary.

REGULATION 118

This deals with offences committed by blowing the horn of a vehicle in certain circumstances; again this attacks noise.

(a) On a restricted road (between 2330 and 0700hrs), i.e. a road with a street lighting system with lamps less than 200 yards apart, or where there is a speed limit other than motorway speed limits.
(b) While the vehicle is stationary, unless there is danger from another moving vehicle.

Note: Theft warning devices, instruments used on the vehicle for advertising goods for sale, and sirens and twin-tones on emergency vehicles do not have to comply with (a) and (b) above.

REGULATION 119

Creates the offence of not being in a position to have proper control of the vehicle, an offence which has caused dispute on numerous occasions, and in many circumstances would take a lot of proving.

Certain situations are obviously breaches of this regulation, but the regulation as a whole centres around the word 'control' and that the driver shall be in such position to have a full view of the road and traffic ahead.

It depends entirely on the set of circumstances at the time. It is conclusive that where a driver is in the ridiculous position of sitting back-to-front in a moving vehicle, then he cannot comply with this regulation – and in any case would perhaps be wandering all over the road. However, at the other end of the scale, for some reason the driver could be holding the steering wheel with one hand yet be in perfect control of the vehicle. A case is known to the author where a motor cyclist was riding 'side saddle', and Magistrates considered that no offence had been committed.

REGULATION 120 – REVERSING

Before reversing your vehicle, make sure that the time and distance involved do not cause inconvenience to other traffic on the road.

If you reverse, say, past an entrance into which you could have backed so as to turn the vehicle and drive forwards, then an offence is complete. In other words, as soon as possible turn the vehicle and drive forwards in the required direction instead of reversing over a distance.

REGULATION 122 – OBSTRUCTION

Unnecessary obstruction doesn't need the vehicle to be parked on a restricted parking area; on any road at any time you could commit an offence if your vehicle obstructs.

REGULATION 123

This requires drivers to park close in to the nearside of the road during the hours of darkness.

There are many exemptions which could be helpful to the HGV driver. It doesn't apply then:

(a) In one-way streets.
(b) In places specially set aside for picking up and setting down passengers.
(c) To vehicles being used on repairs to roads, telephone cables, water-pipes, sewers, and so on.
(d) While a vehicle is being used in the course of repairs to another vehicle, or
(e) When given permission by a Police Constable in uniform.

REGULATION 124 – FAILING TO STOP ENGINE

Before a driver quits his vehicle he should apply the parking brake and stop the engine – unless a person licensed to drive such a vehicle remains in it. But there are fairly obvious exemptions, such as:

(a) Vehicles which have to keep motors running to drive apparatus on the vehicle – tippers, concrete mixers, etc., or
(b) To maintain electrical power in the batteries of the vehicle to drive such apparatus.

In these cases it must be ensured that the vehicle is in such a position that no danger is caused to any person. (In other words, if on a gradient or in a similar position, the handbrake must be set although the engine is still required.)

REGULATION 125 – OPENING OF VEHICLE DOOR

Opening, or permitting to be opened, any door of a vehicle or trailer and causing injury or danger to any person is an offence.

Remember: If your passenger opens a door he commits the offence and you the driver would most likely permit it. Two for the price of one!

REGULATION 126 – TRAILER BRAKE APPLICATION

All this regulation really requires is that if a vehicle is towing a trailer and the trailer is fitted with brakes, *other than over-run brakes*, the driver shall be in a position to be able to apply the trailer brakes – or *another competent person* is in a position to apply the brakes.

What is important, but often overloked, is a little proviso which lets out broken-down vehicles under tow. No-one is required to ride in the broken-down vehicle to apply the brakes provided that it cannot be steered by its own steering gear.

On the same subject, almost:

REGULATION 127

Requires a driver, when leaving a trailer detached from the towing unit, either to apply the parking brake *or* chain at least one wheel.

REGULATION 128

If a trailer is being towed by means of a *rope and chain* then the distance between the nearest points of the towing vehicle and trailer shall not exceed 4.5 m.

If the length of *any means* (rope,chain or tow-bar) exceeds 1.5 m it has to be made clearly visible from both sides of both vehicles. Using orange-coloured rope would satisfy this requirement, but a black-coloured chain would have to be marked with, say, a piece of white material.

Remember: Towing by rope or chain would perhaps occur only with an immediate broken-down vehicle. But *anything* being towed is a *trailer*.

REGULATION 142

This deals with mascots, and says that if a mascot on any part of a vehicle has a projection from it, then an offence of fitting a mascot has been committed. If a projection from a mascot is *likely* to injure any person with whom the vehicle collides then 'remove it' is the advice.

The practice of fitting wheel discs to grills as decoration is debatable, but if there is no projection on the disc it is presumed legal since another part of the vehicle would be first to strike a person with whom it collides.

A good case to refer to is where a manufacturer fitted to certain vehicle models an abstract metal badge depicting a flying bird with beak outstretched beyond the vehicle bonnet. It was held to be 'dangerous parts' and not a dangerous mascot. The word 'mascot' seems possibly to have a magic meaning associated with luck.

It is emphasised that whatever badge or decoration is fitted, if it is considered to be *dangerous* it is an offence under either 'dangerous parts' or 'mascots' regulations.

REGULATION 143

One can install a television set in an HGV provided that the screen, either directly *or by reflection*, is not visible to the driver while he is *in his driving seat*. The vehicle doesn't have to be moving – the regulation applies equally whether the vehicle is stationary on a motorway service area or moving.

Even to install one in a vehicle in a position contrary to the provisions of the regulation is an offence, so all is quiet on the manufacturer's side, as an added extra.

REGULATION 145 – TESTING OF BRAKES, LIGHTS, TYRES, STEERING GEAR, SILENCERS

This is a rather important regulation which is likely to affect an operator or owner/driver. But when one thinks of 'testing' of vehicles, perhaps it is easy to think of it only in the context of the plating and the annual testing regulations which result in a certificate being issued.

For the driver of an HGV it is even easier to remember by the occasional roadside checks where, as a routine check, the Department of Transport and the Police carry out the examination of those items mentioned. Again, this is slightly different, and the power to carry out all these tests comes under a different heading and other sets of legislation.

This regulation, then, deals entirely with the examination of vehicles on *any premises* where the vehicle happens to be.

A Police Officer in uniform, or a person authorised under certain sections of the Road Traffic Act (usually termed 'Department of Transport Examiners' or 'Ministry Examiners'), who has a written authority can examine a vehicle or trailer on *any premises* at *any time*.

If a vehicle or trailer has been involved in a traffic accident then that vehicle or trailer can be examined without consent of its owner.

In all other circumstances, where the vehicle is *on premises*, consent of the owner of the vehicle or trailer has to be obtained. If, however, he refuses to consent to the examination all the authorities have to do is deliver a written notice to the owner giving 48 hours' notice. This notice can be sent by post (in which case 72 hours' notice is allowed), or served personally, or left at the owner's address.

REGULATIONS 147, 151

Every goods vehicle which has been plated and tested must display the plate in the cab. It must be kept readable and in an accessible position. Likewise, a trailer which has been plated and tested must display the test date disc on the nearside, again always readable and accessible. In both cases the plate must be visible from the nearside of the road.

Gross weights and axle weights are not to be in excess of those shown on the relevant columns of the plate.

REGULATION 152

Requires that the braking efficiencies, as listed on page 24, are capable of being produced when the total weight transmitted to the road surface is equal to the design gross weight of the vehicle.

To this end it is practice that during brake tests at testing stations, simulated load torque is placed on each and every wheel to ensure that the minimum required efficiencies are met. This test must always be carried out against the design weights and not the Department of Transport plated weights. This will ensure that the load simulation is up to the maximum the vehicle was designed to carry.

In other words, it would be much against the intention of the regulation if, say, a 16-tonne rigid plated down to 7.5 tonnes to enable the operator to employ an ordinary licence holder, was to have a load torque of only 7.5 tonnes placed on it, when the design weight is 16 tonnes.

REGULATION 153

Says simply that whatever Regulation 152 alters, the original braking requirements must always be complied with if the brakes are tested when running without a load.

Also, that any HGV from new until its first anniversary can have or alter any braking system so long as efficiency requirements are maintained.

REGULATION 154 – TYRES

All axles of goods vehicles are to be equipped with tyres which are designed strengthwise to support adequately the design weight of the axle. The list of tyre sizes in relation to permitted weights is considerable and when coupled with ply ratings and the class into which the vehicle falls, it is felt that a printed list would be too vast.

With regard to size, manufacturers build their tyres to comply with this regulation, whether they be radials or cross-ply tyres.

Radials are marked either 'R' or 'radial', or the identification is set out in the size, for example radials are always maximum-ply rating unless otherwise stated on the tyre.

Cross-plies are not usually identified but most carry a ply rating.

Examples for guidance at testing stations on the above tyre requirements are as follows:

  (i) 900×20 size tyre 14-ply on an axle of a vehicle in Class 2B (unrestricted use): maximum weight is 9150 kg.
 (ii)   The same tyre on an axle of a vehicle in class 2J (restricted to 40 mph and within a 25-mile radius of base): maximum weight on axle 10 170 kg.
(iii)   Older vehicles have a Class GP1 (restricted to 40 mph, but no radius): maximum weight on axle 9180 kg.
 (iv)   The same tyre size (900×20 but only 12-ply) on a 2B class would be down-plated to 8130 kg.

Chapter 2

MOVEMENT OF WIDE AND LONG LOADS UNDER CONSTRUCTION AND USE REGULATIONS 1978

(1) It is important at the outset to bear in mind the magical number of 32 520 kg. This is the maximum gross weight that a vehicle can transmit to the road surface while operating under the *Construction and Use Regulations.*

This maximum weight carries great significance when one is attempting to prove an offence when a load is being moved under the *Special Types Order* (see Chapter 3).

(2) The movement of a large and heavy load applies to its:
    (a) Width   (d) Overall length
    (b) Rearward projection   (e) Weight
    (c) Forward projection

Height is not restricted but occasionally it affects movement.

(3) An 'abnormal load' can be defined as 'a load which cannot without undue expense or risk of damage be divided into two or more loads for the purpose of carriage on roads'.

(4) Under the *Construction and Use Regulations, normally*:
    (a) The maximum width of a vehicle and load is 2.9 m.
    (b) The maximum lateral overhang of the load is .305 m.
    (c) The maximum forward projection of the load is 1.83 m.
    (d) The maximum rearward projection of the load is 1.07 m.
    (e) The maximum gross weight of a vehicle is 32 520 kg. This is the maximum and does not mean that all *Construction and Use* vehicles can carry 32 520 kg. All goods vehicles are plated either by the Department of the Environment or the manufacturers as to their maximum gross and axle weights, but again the maximum is 32 520 kg.

(5) If any of (a), (b), (c) or (d) in (4) above are exceeded with a *Construction and Use* vehicle, some or all Paragraphs of the eighth Schedule to the *Construction and Use Regulations* apply; (e) cannot be exceeded while the vehicle is being used within the requirements of the *Construction and Use Regulations*. These paragraphs are:

    (i) At least two clear days notification to the Chief Officer of Police for each county the load is intended to travel through, giving full details of load, vehicle, and proposed route.

   (ii) Details of attendants, other than the driver,being carried to attend to the load, etc.

  (iii) In the event of forward and rearward projections, pre-scribed marker boards to side and to front/rear of the projection must be fixed.

  (iv) Enable any projection to be easily distinguishable.

At this point it is important to mention again the height of the load. The notice to the Chief Officer of Police is collated and if the load is over 14' height then one would inform local telephone and power cable authorities who have special units to lift telephone wires and power cables etc., and are in attendance throughout the movement.

(6) The amounts by which (4) (a), (b), (c) and (d) can be legally increased are:

  (a) To a maximum width of 4.3 m for load and vehicle.

  (b) If the load and vehicle exceeds 2.9 m but does not exceed 3.5 m – Paragraph (i) of Schedule 8 must be complied with.

  (c) If the load and vehicle exceeds 3.5 m but does not exceed 4.3 m – Paragraphs (i) and (ii) of Schedule 8 must be complied with.

  (d) Forward and rearward load projections: If a forward projection exceeds 1.83 m but does not exceed 3.05 m – Paragraphs (ii) and (iii) of Schedule 8 must be complied with.

  (e) If a rearward projection exceeds 1.07 m but not 1.83 m – Paragraph (iv) of Schedule 8 must be complied with.

  (f) If a rearward projection exceeds 1.83 m but does not exceed 3.05 m – Paragraph (iii) of Schedule 8 must be complied with.

  (g) If a rearward or forward projection exceeds 3.05 m – Paragraphs (i), (ii) and (iii) of Schedule 8 must be complied with.

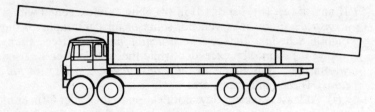

(a) Total laden weight not to exceed 32 520 kg
(b) Maximum length – vehicle and load – 27.4 m
(c) Maximum width – vehicle and load – 4.3 m
(d) If a vehicle and load exceeds 18.3 m in length:
    Police and attendant – yes
Note: For forward/rearward overhang, refer to Figure 20.
    For width overhang, refer to Figure 21.

Figure 17 Vehicle and load weight, length and width limits

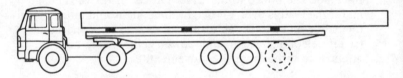

(a) Must comply with conditions (a) (b) (c) in Figure 17
(b) If trailer and load exceed 18.3 m in length:
    Police and attendant – yes
(c) If vehicle, trailer and load exceed 25.9 m:
    Police and attendant – yes

Figure 18 Artic and load weight, length and width limits

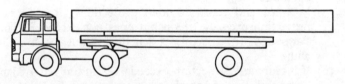

(a) If an articulated vehicle not *normally* used to carry indivisible loads is used to carry such loads, and if this vehicle and load exceed 16.8 m:
    Police must be notified of movement
(b) Remember to keep within plated weight limits
(c) If the vehilce and trailer are not *normally* used for the carriage of indivisible loads, then maximum length of vehicle and trailer not to exceed 15 m

Figure 19 Artic carrying indivisible load

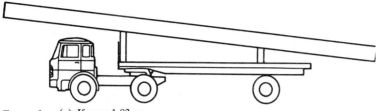

Forward: (a) If over 1.83 m:
           Police – no: attendant – yes
           Marker-boards, end and each side of overhang – yes
      (b) If over 3.05 m:
           Police and attendant – yes
           Marker-boards, end and each side of overhang – yes
      (c) If over 4.5 m:
           Police and attendant – yes
           Marker-boards, end and each side of overhang – yes
           Side ones every 2.4 m

Rearward: (d) If over 1.07 m:
           Must be made easily seen
           Police and attendant – no
      (e) If over 1.83 m:
           Police and attendant – no
           Marker-boards, end of overhang – yes
           If overhang over 3 m, each side – yes
      (f) If over 3.05 m:
           Police and attendant – yes
           Marker-boards, end and each side of overhang – yes
      (g) If over 5.1 m:
           Police and attendant – yes
           Marker-boards, end and each side of overhang – yes
           Side ones every 3.6 m
     Note: Marker board shapes and sizes are illustrated in Figure 22

Figure 20 Forward and rearward load overhang

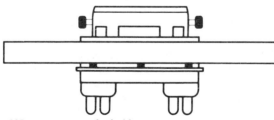

(a) If over 305 mm on *one* or *both* sides:
    Police – yes: attendant – no
(b) If overhang of load *plus* width of vehicle exceeds 2.9 m:
    Police – yes: attendant – no
(c) If overhang of load *plus* width of vehicle exceeds 3.5 m:
    Police and attendant – yes

Figure 21 Width overhang of load

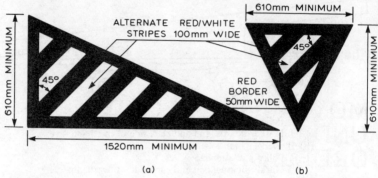

Figure 22 Marker boards for (a) side and (b) forward/rearward overhang of abnormal loads

If an articulated vehicle, the length of which is 15 m or less, is used to carry an indivisible load, and is not constructed and normally used for the carriage of abnormal loads, and together with rearward and forward projections, exceeds 16.8 m – Paragraph (i) of Schedule 8 must be complied with.

(7) I have for the first time just mentioned 'articulated vehicles', the definition of which is 'a heavy motor car or motor car with a trailer so attached to the drawing vehicle that part of the trailer is superimposed upon the drawing vehicle (fifth wheel), and when the trailer is uniformly loaded not less than 20% of the weight of the load is borne by the drawing vehicle.

Under *Construction and Use Regulations*, an articulated vehicle must not exceed 15 m in length unless it is constructed and normally used for the carriage of indivisible loads. If it is so constructed and used, then it can extend to 18.3 m. But in determining what the word 'normally' means, it has been recorded that 44 loads out of 177 were held to be not 'normally used'.

(8) These are the condensed practical dimensions and weights of abnormal loads that can be moved under *Construction and Use Regulations*. No offences are created by Schedule 8, but if a haulier fails to comply with the requirements of the Schedule, the offence is then scavenged from **Regulation 139**, which is the 'long-and-wide' regulation.

(9) *Figures 17* to *21* set out the maximum dimensions and widths of abnormal loads which can be legally moved under *Construction and Use Regulations*. *Figure 22* illustrates warning marker boards to be fixed on the front, rear and sides of overhanging loads.

Chapter 3

MOVEMENT OF LOADS UNDER SPECIAL TYPES ORDER 1979

(1) This Order simply permits certain types of special vehicle to be used on the road which cannot comply in all respects with the *Construction and Use Regulations*.

Let's first of all go to one end of the scale and take a Chieftain tank as an example. Well, a tank runs on tracks, not pneumatic tyres, and tracks in this category are not catered for in the *Construction and Use Regulations*. Its braking system does not comply with the *Construction and Use Regulations*, but the Secretary of State authorises its use on the roads. At the other end of the scale are grass-cutting machines and hedge trimmers – albeit they may be controlled by pedestrians they are *Special Types* vehicles.

(2) It is the obscure vehicles in the *Special Types Order* which one should disregard and not consider as everyday likelihoods. A list of these will probably be helpful:

   (i) Track-laying vehicles.
  (ii) Naval and military vehicles.
 (iii) RNLI vehicles.
 (iv) Grass cutters, hedge trimmers.
  (v) Pedestrian-controlled road maintenance vehicles.
 (vi) Vehicles used for experiment (anti-skid vehicles).
 (vii) Straddle carriers.
(viii) Harvesters.
 (ix) Hay balers.
  (x) Vehicles for moving excavated materials.
 (xi) Vehicles fitted with moving platforms.
 (xii) Engineering plant.

The foregoing vehicles are specially manufactured, and unless perhaps you get made up a one-off special vehicle to do a special job, it is unusual that the Order is not complied with.

If there should be any doubt about the above list then the Order would have to be consulted.

(3) Vehicles which are of concern are those which are grouped under one heading: Article 20 of the *Special Types Order*, 'vehicles used for carrying or drawing abnormal indivisible loads'.

These vehicles are simply ordinary load-carrying vehicles or trailers but specially-built in relation to springs, tyres, brakes and power-to-weight ratio, and have a laden weight in excess of 32 520 kg or loads over 4.3 m wide.

(4) These specially-built vehicles are plated by the manufacturers as to their maximum design weights, but they carry no special notice to indicate that they are *Special Types* vehicles.

The maximum permitted dimensions under the *Special Types Order* are:

Length	27.4 m
Width	6.1 m
Weight	152 400 kg
Wheel weight	11 430 kg

(5) Such vehicles are exempted from the *Plating and Testing Regulations*, but an operator who uses his vehicles to transport an abnormal load to a destination can bring back a return load on that vehicle, but he must comply with these two provisos:
   (a) Load not to exceed 32 520 kg, and
   (b) Must be plated and tested by the Department of Transport, which will restrict him to the above maximum weight.

(6) In respect of the load being indivisible, in *certain cases* 'indivisible' is stretched to mean either:
   (a) Where one abnormal indivisible load is carried, the vehicle can carry articles of a *similar character*, or
   (b) To carry more than one abnormal indivisible load, each being of the *same character* as the other(s).

Figures 23 and *25* will assist in explaining this proviso, and *Figures 24, 26, 27* and *28* will be useful in ascertaining the various dimensions and weights, and combinations of vehicles which undertake the carriage of abnormal loads.

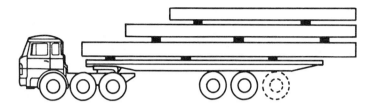

(a) If maximum weight is under 32 520 kg, vehicle or combination can carry:
    (i) More than one abnormal load of the *same character*, or
    (ii) One abnormal load and any articles of a *similar character*
    Concrete beams are a good example – different sizes can be carried on the same load
(b) If maximum weight exceeds 32 520 kg but does not exceed 76 200 kg, then vehicle or combination can carry more than one load of the *same character*
(c) All loads must be loaded at the same site and taken to the same delivery site.
(d) Also, must comply with conditions (a) (c) (d) (e) (f) (g) (i) in Figure 26

Figure 23 Vehicle or combination carrying more than one indivisible load

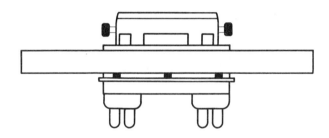

(a) *Generally*, 4.3 m
(b) This width can be extended to 6.1 m, but if 4.3 m is exceeded special permission to move must be obtained. See Appendix for procedure
(c) If width is over 2.9 m:
    Police – yes: attendant – no
(d) If width is over 3.5 m:
    Police and attendant – yes

Note: Wide loads of up to 6.1 m can be carried on ordinary Construction and Use vehicles if the *total* laden weight is under 32 520 kg, but it must comply with the Special Types Order in relation to Police, attendants, speed limits and special authority

Figure 24 Width restrictions on all types of vehicle and combination include the width of the complete vehicle and load

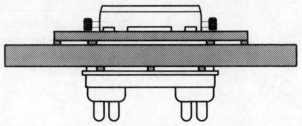

Must comply with width restriction in Figure 24(a) and conditions (b) (c) (d) in Figure 23

Special notes: Forward/rearward load overhang can usually be catered for and carried under Construction and Use.

If the vehicle fully laden exceeds 32 520 kg it has to be designed to that excess weight and move under the Special Types Order

Figure 25 Vehicle carrying one indivisible load plus a second indivisible load of the same character

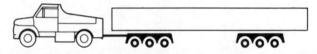

(a) Maximum length – 27.4 m
(b) Maximum weight – 152 400 kg
(c) Maximum wheel weight – 11 430 kg
(d) Maximum width – vehicle and load – 4.3 m
(e) This width can be extended to 6.1 m, but if 4.3 m is exceeded then special permission to move must be obtained. See Appendix for procedure
(f) If combination exceeds 25.9 m in length:
      Police and attendant – yes
(g) If trailers plus load exceed 18.3 m in length:
      Police and attendant – yes
(h) If weight exceeds 76 200 kg:
      Police and bridge authority – yes
(i) If weight is less than 76 200 kg, but axle weight exceeds 11 430 kg:
      Police – no: bridge authority – yes

Figure 26 Special Types Order load-carrying vehicles, gross weight exceeding 32 520 kg. Locomotive with bogies – two trailers, carrying load on more than one vehicle

(7) All vehicles operating under the *Special Types Order* must comply with rigid movement details, by notifying:

(a) The Police in the case of length, width and weight (see (i) in *Figure 26*), and

(b) The highways and bridges authorities in respect of weight.

(a) Maximum length – 27.4 m
(b) Maximum weight – 152 400 kg
(c) Maximum wheel weight – 11 430 kg
(d) Maximum width – vehicle and load – 4.3 m
(e) This width can be extended to 6.1 m, but if 4.3 m is exceeded, special permission to move must be obtained. See Appendix for procedure
(f) If combination exceeds 25.9 m in length:
    Police and attendant – yes
(g) Note: Driver of 'pusher' vehicle is *not* an attendant
(h) Conditions (h) (i) in Figure 26 must be complied with

Figure 27 Push-pull locomotives with rigid trailer – carrying load on one vehicle

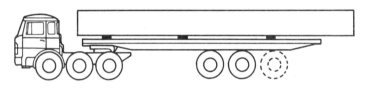

Conditions (a) to (i) in Figure 26 must be complied with

Figure 28 Artic maximum combination lengths and widths

For certain weights a form of indemnity (*Figure 29*) must be taken out by the hauliers.

If any of the details contained in the notice of movement (*Figure 30*) are not complied with, the vehicle is automatically lifted from the *Special Types Order* and placed back into the *Construction and Use Regulations*, and then it must comply with those regulations in all respects. But the most important point to prove is the gross weight – and the vehicle and load must be put onto a weighbridge to ascertain this.

(8) Attendants must be carried in these cases:
   (a) On any vehicle where forward or rearward projection together with the vehicle exceeds 18.3 m overall.
   (b) Where lateral overhang on one or both sides exceeds 3.5 m.

Form of Indemnity

I/We hereby agree to indemnify you and each and every highway or bridge authority responsible for the maintenance and repair of any road or bridge on the journey to which the above notice relates in respect of any damage which may be caused to any such road or bridge—

(*a*) by [any of] the above mentioned vehicle[s]—

(i) by reason of the construction of or weight transmitted to the road surface by [any of] the said vehicle[s], or

(ii) by reason of the dimensions, distribution or adjustment of the load carried by [any of] the said vehicle[s]; or

(*b*) by any other vehicle by reason of the use of [any of] the above-mentioned vehicle[s] on the road or, as the case may be, the bridge except to the extent that the damage was caused or contributed to by the negligence of the driver of the other vehicle:

Provided that any claim in respect of damage so caused by any vehicle shall be made in writing within twelve months from the date on which the vehicle is last used on the journey to which the above notice relates, stating the occasion and place of the damage.

Date....................................   Signed................................

Note:—Paragraph (*a*)(ii) above only applies where vehicles are carrying an abnormal indivisible load and in other cases should be omitted.

Figure 29 Form of indemnity

(c) Any combination which has a forward and rearward projection which, together with the vehicle, exceeds 25.9 m overall.

(d) Articles 20 or 21 – vehicle which has forward projection exceeding 1.83 m or rearward projection exceeding 3.05 m must carry at least one attendant.

(9) Marker boards (*Figure 22*) as prescribed in Paragraph (iii), Schedule 8, (Section (5) of Chapter 2), of the *Construction and Use Regulations* must be fitted to the load as follows:

(a) On any forward or rearward projection exceeding 1.83 m, or

(b) Where a rearward projection exceeds 1.07 m but does not exceed 1.83 m.

(10) If moving a load under Article 20, notice to Chief Officer of Police has to be given, with at least two days notice, in the following circumstances:

(a) If the vehicle together with load exceeds 2.9 m in width.

(b) If the overall length of the vehicle, including any forward or rearward projection of its load, exceeds 18.3 m.

(c) Any vehicle with a forward or rearward projection exceeding 3.05 m.

(d) Any combination of vehicles and trailers, which together with any forward or rearward projections, exceeds 25.9 m overall.

Form of Notice to Police and to Highway and Bridge Authorities.
THE MOTOR VEHICLES (AUTHORISATION OF SPECIAL TYPES)
GENERAL ORDER, 1979

(Subject to the prior agreement of each of the authorities to which this notice is sent, it may be used to give notice of additional journeys, different vehicles, routes and destinations.)

List of all Police Forces, Highway and Bridge Authorities to which this form is sent.

Operator	Telephone No.
Address	Telex No.
	Operator's Licence No.
	Operator's Reference No.

In pursuance of Article(s) of the above mentioned Order, I/we being the operator of the undermentioned vehicle(s) to which the Order applies, hereby give notice that it is my/our intention to use the said vehicle(s) on the roads specified below. The route and Department of Transport Classification numbers proposed to be used are:

PARTICULARS OF JOURNEY

FROM (full address)	TIME AND DATE	via

TO (full address)	TIME AND DATE

PARTICULARS OF LOAD

LOAD PROFILE (rough sketch showing outline of laden vehicle from front or rear. This to be omitted if sent by telex).

Registration No. of vehicle (or substitute)	Type of vehicle	DESCRIPTION OF LOAD

PARTICULARS OF VEHICLE

Overall length of vehicle		Projection —front		Projection —rear		Total length	

Overall width		Maximum height		Gross weight or Gross train weight	

No. of wheels per axle							
Axle weight							
Axle spacing							

Figure 30 Notice of movement

    (e) Any articulated vehicle, or vehicle drawing one trailer, which, together with any forward or rearward projection of the load, exceeds 18.3 m overall.

    (f) Where the gross weight of any vehicle and load, or combination of vehicles and load, exceeds 76 200 kg.

(11) *Notice to bridge authorities*: This must be given:

    (a) If load exceeds 76 200 kg, and

    (b) Where axle weights exceed those permitted by the *Construction and Use Regulations*.

In respect of notice to Police and bridge authorities of intention to move, Saturdays and Sundays do not count for the purposes of periods of notice. It is essential to notify within the prescribed period.

(12) *Speed limits*: Any vehicle authorised by Article 20:

    (a) Which is not carrying a load,

    (b) Where the *vehicle* does not exceed 2.9 m, and

    (c) Complies with *Construction and Use Regulations* requirements in respect of brakes, springs, wings and tyres,

speed not to exceed 20 mph, but in any other case 12 mph. Motorways 60 mph, but if a vehicle exceeds 4.3 m width, it is limited to 20 mph on all roads.

(13) Engineering plant and hybrid vehicles are the only things to discuss, other than Article 20 vehicles.

Engineering plant, which includes mobile cranes, must be over 4.3 m wide or exceeding 76 200 kg before they need to comply with anything. Such machinery is not to be confused with load-carrying vehicles.

Hybrid vehicles, such as dumper trucks, racing cars, etc., have been held not to be motor vehicles, therefore they are exempt from long and wide load regulations.

(14) *Escorts*: The fact that a load is abnormal does not automatically mean that it has to be escorted by Police patrols. The need to escort differs from one Police area to another, depending perhaps on changing road features (for example, road works), bridge weight restrictions, or the like. But when the load, in relation to weights or projections, enters the magnum bracket, then it is usual to have Police escorts through all Police areas.

(15) All load-carrying vehicles, plated as *Special Type* vehicles, are covered by the foregoing, whether they are flatbeds, articulated outfits or locomotive tractor units towing trailers. The only restriction which differs concerns articulated trailers – in this case they must not exceed 2.9 m in width unless used laden as part of an outfit with a gross weight not exceeding 50 000 kg.

FOR QUICK REFERENCE:

Special notes about wide, long and heavy loads whether operating under the *Construction and Use Regulations* or the *Special Types Order*

(a) If the load and vehicle gross more than 32 520 kg, then the operator must comply with the *Special Types Order* requirements (attendants, notification, speed limits).

(b) When anticipating a load in excess of 32 520 kg, then check on the design weight of the vehicle. If the vehicle plate permits exceeding this limit then the load can be carried. But a vehicle cannot simply load over its plated weight maximum (Department of Transport plate) and then operate without the authority of the *Special Types Order*.

(c) Vehicles of a special type are plated by the manufacturer and *not* by the Department of Transport. Such vehicles are exempt from the *Plating and Testing Regulations*, but if the operator subjects them to the Department of Transport test, then such vehicles, having delivered a load under *Special Types Order*, can have a return load of any commodity and run under ordinary *Construction and Use Regulations*.

(d) Basically, the *Special Types Order* simply allows an indivisible load of a *heavy nature* to be hauled by a vehicle which, mainly because of its dimensions, cannot comply with the requirements of *Construction and Use Regulations*. As far as wide and long loads are concerned then unless it is intended to exceed a gross weight of 32 520 kg, or haul a load in excess of 4.3 m wide, then it can be hauled and only the requirements of the *Construction and Use Regulations* apply.

(e) If operating under *Special Types Order*, and gross weight does not exceed 76 200 kg, and *there is no other abnormality*, then Police *do not* have to be notified, but road and bridge authorities *do*.

(f) The maximum weight limit that can be moved under *Special Types Order* is 152 400 kg gross, unless special permission is given to exceed this weight (see details in the Appendix to this Chapter).

(g) A Special Types vehicle can carry more than one abnormal load (i) if the laden vehicle weight does not exceed 32 520 kg. The loads must be of the *same* character, and any articles of a *similar* character can be carried at the same time (useful for lightweight abnormally long and/or wide loads). (ii) If the laden vehicle weight exceeds 32 520 kg, then by carrying one abnormal load it can carry others of the *same* character up to a laden weight of 76 200 kg.

APPENDIX

PROCEDURE TO MOVE *EXCEPTIONAL* LOAD (VR1)

The Department of Transport is the only authority to issue permission to move any vehicle and load in excess of the dimensions mentioned in the foregoing paragraphs on indivisible loads.

Provided that an operator has complied with the correct notification procedure, then in normal circumstances the Police Force headquarters' Abnormal Load Unit will assist with any further advice in respect of safety of other road users.

But any load termed a 'VR1 load' which, because of its massive size, has to be specially authorised, then in the first instance contact:

Department of Transport
BET Division
St Christopher House
Southwark Street   Telephone: 01-928 7999
London SE1 0TE   Telex: 21352

If the intended load is between 4.3 m and 6.1 m wide, but otherwise within the limits, then Extension 3327 will deal.

For loads in excess of all the limits mentioned, ask for Extension 3673.

Chapter 4

THE TACHOGRAPH REGULATIONS 1979

INTRODUCTION

All member countries of the European Community have legislation making compulsory the keeping of goods vehicle and passenger vehicle drivers' records by means of tachographs.

The *Passenger and Goods Vehicles (Recording Equipment) Regulations 1979* brought into line most goods vehicles and passenger-carrying vehicles used in both the United Kingdom and the rest of the EEC countries, and 31 December 1981 marks the end of the old system of 'log books'.

However, a phasing programme designed to avoid saturation at calibration and fitting centres is taking vehicles, in stages, to the operative date of 1 January 1982.

Before entering into detail about the tachograph and its requirements, it is essential to list the types of vehicle to which compulsory fitting applies. They are:

(a) All public service vehicles of whatever weight or capacity.
(b) All passenger-carrying vehicles (which are not public service vehicles) constructed to carry more than 12 passengers.
(c) Heavy locomotives, light locomotives, motor tractors and articulated vehicles. Also included are goods vehicles with a plated weight exceeding 3.5 tonnes or, if not plated, with an unladen weight in excess of 1425 kg.

Vehicles related to the services listed below are exempted from the regulations, (and in any case do not have to be fitted with tachographs), but this does not exempt their drivers from the 'number of hours worked'. Almost all goods-carrying vehicles are subject to 'hours' limits (see Chapter 5).

Gas and electricity	Police, fire and ambulance
Telephone and telegraph	Highway authority
Carrying Post Office mail	Carrying rescue materials
Specialised breakdown	Armed Forces
Radio and television	Water drainage and flood prevention

Also, tractors with a maximum speed of less than 30 mph.

The fitting programme – or phasing table – is important and it seems that perhaps operators will find difficulty in booking their vehicles for fitting at the approved centre during the required period for their particular vehicles.

PHASING TABLE

First registered on or after 1.8.79 but before 1.12.79 must be fitted by 1.6.80
First registered on or after 1.8.78 but before 1.8.79 must be fitted by 1.10.80
First registered on or after 1.8.77 but before 1.8.78 must be fitted by 1.1.81
First registered on or after 1.8.76 but before 1.8.77 must be fitted by 1.3.81
First registered on or after 1.8.75 but before 1.8.76 must be fitted by 1.5.81
First registered on or after 1.8.73 but before 1.8.75 must be fitted by 1.8.81
First registered before   1.8.73   must be fitted by 31.12.81

The instrument

Basically the tachograph is a cable-driven speedometer (*Figure 31*) but it incorporates an electric or mechanical clock and a chart recording mechanism.

It has to be fitted inside the cab of the vehicle – anywhere convenient – but it must remain visible from the driver's seat.

The instrument must be constructed so that it is possible through the operation of a switch to record automatically and separately the following periods of time.

(a) Driving time, or 'time at the wheel',
(b) Other periods of work and of attendance at work – 'on duty' time, and
(c) Breaks from work and rest periods.

Breaking that down further means that the following details are permanently on record:

(i) The speed at which the vehicle is driven,
(ii) The distance travelled,

Figure 31 Lucas Kienzle 1311-27 automatic tachograph

(iii) The distance between stops,
(iv) The total hours of driving time,
 (v) Breaks – rest periods etc., and
(vi) The number of times the tachograph face is opened and closed.

(**N.B.** For your own benefit: Frequent opening and closing should be avoided – a small V is cut in the chart's outer edge on each opening and closing, and if these become numerous, questions could be asked – for example, 'Why?')

Smiths or Lucas Kienzle are the main suppliers of tachographs and single-driver instruments are available. At the other end of the scale sophisticated meters can be fitted which record engine speeds and the like, a facility which assists fleet operators in the economics of their businesses. But whichever tachograph one decides to install it must record details as mentioned in the previous paragraph, and where two-man crews are used an EEC dual-purpose instrument must be fitted (second member must have his chart recording although he is not driving).

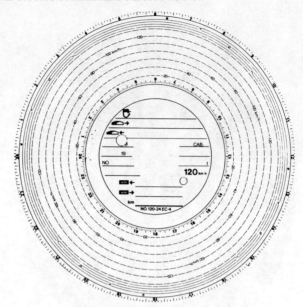

Figure 32 Tachograph one-day chart

Recording and charts

Each chart covers a period of 24 hours and is time-marked around its outside edge by the 24-hour clock method (*Figure 32*).

Three separate stylii (or needles) are incorporated inside the mechanism to record the required details, but the needles do not mark the charts with any form of ink or liquid. The charts are of special paper – red backing with a white chalk surface which the needles simply scratch off to leave a permanent record on the red backing paper.

Another danger risked by unnecessary opening of the chart container! The chalk surface is highly sensitive and even a touch with a fingernail will mark it – if the chart surface is spoilt then the offence of 'no records' is committed.

Centre field

The centre fields – on both front and reverse sides – must contain the following details:

(a) Name of driver
(b) Date
(c) Speedo reading outward

(d) Speedo reading inward
(e) Registration mark of vehicle
(f) Place where journey commenced
(g) Place where journey finished.

So, a driver commencing duty at Exeter and terminating at the end of his tour at Manchester is required to enter only these places – on the centre field – although he may have had a multi-drop load. But his load drops will of course have been recorded on the outer field (see paragraph Chart Analysis, page 61, and *Figure 34*).

Outer field

On the outer field of the chart are recorded all the requirements from (i) to (vi) in the paragraph headed 'The Instrument', pages 54–55.

Time scales

The scale on the outer edge is fairly straightforward, marked off in the 24-hour method at five-minute intervals. Nearer to the centre field is a secondary time-scale band marked identically to the outer scale.

As soon as the tachograph is switched on it starts its recording according to whichever mode it is tuned to, and will keep going until it is switched off. Remember, it is the driver's accurate record of work and it is his responsibility to see that the tachograph is switched on and off and the correct mode selected (see last paragraph of this Chapter for mode symbol explanation).

Speed radial

Working inwards, this is the next item recorded on the outer field. Remember that it keeps an accurate record of the speed of the vehicle at all times – but the author hastens to add that with an offence such as exceeding legal speed limits, then corroborative evidence, other than a tachograph record, must be produced by the Police to prove the offence.

And on the other side of the coin – I would be very surprised if in the future an HGV driver did not at some time produce his tachograph record in his defence of any similar offence! But basically the speed radial record is used by an operator to analyse fuel consumption and wear-and-tear factors. This is perhaps the time to suggest that normally any tachograph record would be required to be produced as evidence only in relation to an offence of a driver's excess hours of work.

Running and stopping times

Remember, then, that immediately the tachograph is switched on it begins to record whatever happens to the vehicle from that time on.

From within a minute of the vehicle moving off, the inner time radial records that movement with a broad continuous line. When the vehicle stops, the time radial is still marking but with a thin continuous line. These actions are termed 'in-scope' and 'out-of-scope driving periods'. Rest periods are also recorded by a thin continuous line in the appropriate mode group on the outer field.

Distance recording

The distance the vehicle travels is also recorded on the outer field and is shown as a set of ∨ lines, thus: ∨∧∨∧∨∧. The needle which records these details reverses direction every five miles, therefore one complete   ∨   equals 10 miles.

Opening and closing of tachograph face

The chart also records the number of times that the tachograph is opened and closed. Each time this is done a V is cut on the outside edge of the chart at the exact time of opening and closing and the needle marks the disc face.

The importance of avoiding doing this frequently has already been stressed on page 55.

Central 'key hole'

The disc is provided with a central 'key hole' (or series of holes) which enables it to be inserted correctly so that the time on the clock and the time on the disc correspond exactly.

Centre field details required – front

To be entered by driver *before inserting disc*:

(a)   First name and surname of crew member

(b)   Place where use of chart begins

(c)   19   Date when use of chart begins

(d)   No: Registration mark of vehicle

(c)   Odometer reading at point of departure
If sleeper cab, mark X

(f)   t   Gross vehicle weight in metric tonnes

To be entered by driver *at end of shift*:

(a)   Place where use of chart ends

(b)   19   Date when chart ends

(c)   Odometer reading of completion of work

(d)   KM   Distance travelled

Reverse side of charts

The recording field of the reverse side (*Figure 33*) is printed in red and should be used in case of mechanical breakdown of the tachograph. It can be hand-written in ink or ball-point. In normal circumstances, if the instrument fails it would be more practical to use the normal diagrammatic type of record book and this is perfectly in order.

If the rear of the chart is used when a vehicle change takes place, due perhaps to breakdown, it will be seen that there is space for three vehicle changes. In each case the following have to be entered:

(a)   Time of vehicle change

(b)   No: Registration number of new vehicle

(c) ⊢⟶   Odometer reading at departure

(d) ⟵⊣   Odometer reading at end of journey

(e)   KM   Distance travelled

Often with fleet operators a driver changes vehicles part way through his duty tour – he then removes his chart from the first vehicle's tachograph and continues in writing on the reverse side when he commences with the new vehicle.

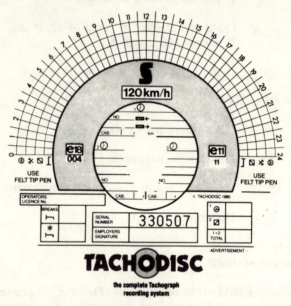

Figure 33 Reverse side of tachograph chart (printed in red and giving space for handwritten entries)

If the illustrations in this chapter are studied in conjunction with the foregoing paragraphs it will soon be seen that all the recording is a delicate operation, but it is done automatically and, except for the centre field entry, needs no help from the driver. When the chart is removed, careful handling is essential.

Discs – general

It was originally intended that all discs should be serial numbered but this is no longer required.

Likewise, a register of disc issues was to have been kept by the operator – this is not now required, but a driver should be issued with discs in convenient batches, say 14 at a time, especially if the driver is to be away from the depot. And, of course, the driver may spoil a disc prior to inserting it in the tachograph – so at least two a day to the driver is reasonable.

The two previous days' records must be carried by the driver but they can be retained by him for up to 21 days. However, the operator must examine and sign the discs within seven days of use.

Chart analysis

Figure 34 shows a chart typical of a day's duty for a driver. You will see that it is basically analysed and shows clearly what is in fact recorded.

If one really wishes to read accurately the details on the disc then investment in a good magnifying glass is essential.

For the operator, accessories are available – static magnifiers, hair-line cursors and the like will give him an accurate record

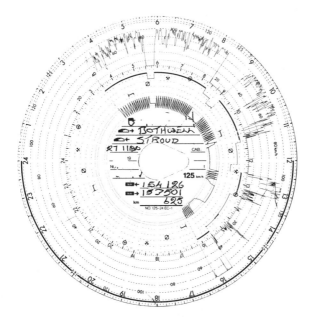

Figure 34 Example of used tachograph chart

which in some circumstances are incredible. Acceleration/deceleration, even the locking of the road wheels (skidding), can be defined from the disc by an expert.

An analyst friend of mine boasts that he can tell when the driver has been for a piddle!

Fitting of instruments

This can only be carried out at a calibration centre authorised by the Department of the Environment.

On fitting it must be marked and sealed in six separate places between the tachograph head and the initial drive link. These seals can be broken only in cases of emergency, repair or re-fitting. In proving any offence in respect of disc records it is essential evidence that all the seals be intact.

When the instrument is installed a plate must be fitted to it bearing the following details:

(a) Name and address of fitter.
(b) Character efficient of the vehicle.
(c) Circumference of the tyres.
(d) The date on which these details were determined.

Examination of the tachograph must be made every two years, but this can be done by the Department of the Environment each year when the vehicle itself is tested. After each check the plate details must be renewed.

Tolerences on the instrument are permitted in respect of:

(a) Distance travelled,
(b) Speed of the vehicle, and
(c) Time recording.

But these tolerences must be read in conjunction with the actual regulations.

Mode symbols

 Means driving time (at the wheel)

 Means all other working periods (including time as second crew member)

 Breaks from work and daily rest periods

 Actual work, other than driving

Chapter 5

GOODS VEHICLE DRIVERS' HOURS OF WORK

The host of legislation and amendments which over the years has controlled the permitted number of hours that goods vehicle drivers may work has caused more problems for everyone connected with such vehicles, from the drivers themselves to the Police who administer its many complications, than the whole of any of the Road Traffic Regulatons put together.

Through the years, mainly because of the increase in the number of vehicles, coupled with inadequate roads and the appalling road accident statistics, the regulations have been gradually altered in many ways to try to reach a happy compromise to suit everyone connected with the operation and driving of goods vehicles.

Most road traffic legislation is produced in an effort to make the roads a safer place to use, but alas it is usually accepted in the wrong context and the next thing that is apparent is that offenders are abusing it.

It is when this misunderstanding creeps into the laws relating to vehicles that problems are caused whereby the administering by authorities becomes that much more difficult.

In many cases drivers and operators think that legislaton is making a good attempt to suppress the use of their vehicles, and a 'them and us' situation arises. But it should be remembered that the basic objective intended by legislators of traffic law is the safety of the driver himself, every other road user and the general public.

Although it was never intended to quote in this book the actual working of sections of regulations, those relating to hours of work have to be an exception. The whole basis of the number of hours worked by HGV drivers is centred on this statement . . . . 'the purpose is to ensure observance of proper hours or periods of work, to protect the public against the risks which arise in cases where HGV drivers are suffering from fatigue'.

If every HGV driver did a quick analysis, there is little doubt that most would agree that the spirit of this legislation is absolutely correct, and it wasn't all that long ago that the 'suffering from fatigue' suggestion had a real meaning. There are very few drivers who have not had a sudden reminder, somehow somewhere on the road, that they are sufferng from fatigue.

The Transport Act 1968 modernised the hours of work as we all knew it for a good number of years, and I do not suppose that drastic alterations would have been made but for that turning point in history when Britain joined the European Economic Community.

It did not take long to realise that vast changes would have to be made within the realms of road transport, least of all having to fall into line with the greater restrictions of the other Continental countries.

The European Economic Community Regulation No EEC/543/ 69 which started all the amendments to and reduction of drivers hours applies to Goods and Passenger Services within (a) the country of origin of the vehicle, (b) the country in which he is working within the EEC and any third country which is governed by AETR regulations.

'AETR' will often appear in material relating to these regulations but the full heading of the agreement is 'The Work of Crews of Vehicles Engaged in International Road Transport'. Hence the useful abbreviation.

It was apparent that before this massive agreement got fully off the ground, as is usual with all Legislation involving major changes there would have to be a transition period. This meant that the requirements would have to be gradually phased in instead of the whole becoming an overnight happening.

Without going further into the whys and wherefores with drivers' hours we come bang up to date, taking us right through the transition period and as from 1 January 1981, starting off with a clean sheet.

It must be emphasised that the new regulations are complicated and it is already admitted that some are not even clear. On some aspects the author has fixed interpretations which can be used only as guide lines. A court of law will, no doubt, eventually settle any of these points which are at present debatable.

Bearing in mind that this entire chapter deals with the number of hours HGV drivers can legally work, it is extremely important always to remember the following points when dealing with hours worked.

These points are, that drivers of all vehicles which are constructed or drastically altered to carry goods or burden ('burden', says the dictionary, means 'load') are brought within the law of drivers' hours. This fact may come as a surprise, but the very few drivers who do not come within the scope of the regulations are these:

(a) Armed Forces,
(b) Fire brigade,
(c) Police, and
(d) Those who drive goods vehicles off the public road.

Even Crown vehicles, such as are used in forestry, are not exempt.

Important: This will be the only part in which drivers of passenger vehicles are referred to, the whole deals solely with goods vehicle drivers. This is only to mention the unusual position of a driver employed both as an HGV driver and passenger-vehicle driver. Here it suffices to say that normally work done with passenger vehicles counts in the build-up of work done with goods vehicles.

In a number of parts of the regulations new words and definitions appear. Some of these are listed below, and they will be found useful to refer to.

Note: These definitions may differ in meaning from those in other acts and regulations.

(a) *Tractor*: Any mechanically self-propelled vehicle circulating on the road (other than a vehicle running on rails) and specially designed to pull, push or move trailers, semi-trailers, implements or machines.
(b) *Trailer*: Any vehicle designed to be coupled to a motor vehicle or tractor.
(c) *Semi-trailer*: A trailer without a front axle, coupled in such a way that a substantial part of its weight and the weight of its load is borne by the tractor or motor vehicle.
(d) *Crew member*: Means the driver or driver's mate.
(e) *Driver*: Any person who drives the vehicle, even for a short period, or who is carried in the vehicle in order to be available for driving if necessary. **Note:** Read this one again!

(f) *Driver's mate*: Any person accompanying the driver of a vehicle in order to assist him in certain manoeuvres and habitually taking an effective part in the transport operations, but not being a driver within the meaning of (e) (minimum age 18 years).

(g) *Rolling week*: Means any period of seven consecutive days.

(h) *Daily rest period*: Any uninterrupted period of at least eight hours during which the crew members may freely dispose of their time and are entirely free to move about as they please.

As we progress through the breaking down of duty periods and driving periods it will be essential to refer to the above definitions in order to arrive at the correct maximum hours of work overall. **Note:** The rolling week is not a legal requirement for a driver engaged solely on National work to add up to his duty limit of 60 hours per week. What the law requires is that he will not be on duty in any fixed week for more than 60 hours.

But as the rolling week applies to *all driving time* and *rest periods* it is easier to use the rolling week for adding up the *weekly duty limit*. However, doing it this way results in applying slightly more requirements, but one will then always be within the law.

For drivers who mix National with Domestic driving there is no choice – you have to use the rolling week because the maximum duty cannot exceed 60 hours.

With the hope of simplifying matters, categories of drivers and vehicles will be dealt with here in four separate Sections: (I) NATIONAL, (II) INTERNATIONAL, (III) DOMESTIC, (IV) MIXED DRIVING. So, refer to each Section and under the first paragraph, or definition, each driver will find if this particular area of the regulations fits him and his vehicle use.

Under some Sections there are exemptions – if a vehicle is exempt from the rules under one, it will have to comply with the rules under another.

SECTION I – NATIONAL

Rules applying inside the UK.
Maximum authorised laden/unladen vehicle-weight exceeding 3.5 tonnes.

BASIC HOURS LIMITS

Daily driving   8 hours

This is time actually spent at the wheel, between daily rest periods. Nine hours working is permitted twice per week except by drivers of (a) vehicles or tractors with one trailer totalling in excess of 20 tonnes, (b) vehicles or tractors with more than one trailer.
Remember: This does not increase the weekly hours limit.

Daily duty   11 hours with 12½ hours spreadover

But the excess over 11 hours must be spent off duty.
Note: If a driver does not exceed four hours driving a day he is exempt from daily duty, weekly duty and spreadover limits for that week. A 'day' for this purpose is 24 hours starting at midnight.

A 'driver' who does not drive is exempt from daily duty and spreadover limits. On non-driving days the first 11 hours of duty count towards the weekly duty limit.

If a vehicle with two drivers has a bunk, this can spread over 22 hours. If not fitted with a bunk, it is reduced to 17 hours. But any 'on duty' time above 11 hours is not to involve active work.

Daily spreadover   12½ hours

Daily rest   11 hours

At any time while at work a driver must take 11 hours rest during the past 24 hours.
Remember: Rest cannot be taken on the vehicle unless a bunk is fitted and the vehicle is stationary.
Note: Daily rest can be reduced in hours in the following circumstances: Twice in a week 11 hours can be reduced to nine hours when rest is taken at the vehicle base, or eight hours if taken away from base, or to one of each of eight and nine hours. BUT, the lost time must be compensated.

Vehicles which have two drivers and a bunk: A driver, each time he is on duty, must have eight hours continuous rest in the past 30 hours. If the vehicle has no bunk it is 10 hours in the last 27 hours.

If the vehicle is operating within 50km of base and used in connection with harvesting transport, for 30 days of any year the rest period can be reduced from 11 to 10 hours daily.

The rest period can be split into two, but only in circumstances which include a ferry crossing. A bunk has to be available during both parts of the rest period, though when one part is taken on the ferry the second part must be increased by two hours and taken immediately before or after joining or leaving the ferry.

Weekly driving   48 hours   Fortnightly driving   92 hours

Bearing in mind that the rolling week is any period of seven consecutive days (see definition) it means that from any given time when a driver is on duty he must keep within the limits looking back over the past 168 hours. The same applies to the fortnightly limit, which is any period of 14 consecutive days.

Weekly duty   60 hours

Weekly rest   29 hours

A week as mentioned previously, this is any period of seven consecutive days. This period must be taken immediately before or after a daily rest period, in one uninterrupted break.

If required, five hours of weekly rest can be taken off with any daily rest period in the same week.

Continuous driving   4 hours

Self-explanatory really, and means any unbroken period of actual driving time.

Remember: This does not apply to drivers who keep within 50km radius of base. If the limit is reached then a break must be taken. See *Continuous duty* next.

Continuous duty   5½ hours

A ½-hour break must be taken by a driver after 5½ hours continuous duty. This ½-hour break may be split into two

20-minute breaks or three 15-minute breaks, spread out over and immediately following the maximum duty period or the continuous driving period. But this spreadover concession will not apply to (a) vehicles and tractors with one trailer totalling over 20 tonnes, and (b) vehicles and tractors with more than one trailer.

The drivers of these vehicles must take one hour off after the driving limit, or two ½-hour breaks between start and finish of the driving day.

Note: If by splitting the break the continuous driving limit is exceeded, then the break must be taken as one whole hour.

Breaks   ½ hour

Mileage limits

On certain HGVs there is also a distance limit as well as a time limit on daily driving.

These vehicles are (a) a motor vehicle or tractor with more than one trailer and semi-trailer, (b) a motor vehicle or tractor with one trailer or semi-trailer and a maximum total weight in excess of 20 tonnes.

Unless these types of vehicle, (a) and (b), are either (i) double-crewed or (ii) fitted with a tachograph, then they are restricted to 450 km a day.

But that driver can drive vehicles not mentioned in (i) and (ii) above either before or afterwards, but he must still comply with the daily rest period.

Remember: The continuous driving period cannot be extended but *in emergencies* the distance limit, the daily hours limit, the weekly driving hours limit and the daily rest requirements can be broken in the following circumstances:

(a) In case of danger, or in circumstances beyond the driver's control.

(b) To render assistance, as a result of breakdown, to the extent necessary to ensure the safety of persons or the load of the vehicle.

(c) To enable the driver to reach a safe stopping place or, depending on circumstances, the end of his journey.

Special cases

These sometimes occur, and details will be found as an Appendix to this Chapter.

Bonus payments

These payments, where they affect miles or the amount of load carried, cannot be paid where doing so would endanger road safety.

Exemptions

Exemptions from this Section

Remember: If the use of your vehicle comes into one of the Section I exemptions it is still restricted; it simply falls into another Section use.

Vehicles exempted are those used by:

    Civil Defence
    Drainage and flood-prevention authorities
    Water, gas, electricity services
    Post Office (mail carriage)
    Telephone services
    Highway authorities
    Refuse collection
    Radio, television and detection vans
    Other public-authority vehicles used for public services

provided that none of the above is in competition with professional road hauliers.

Note: Vehicles on contract from private firms to exempted authorities are not exempt from this Section unless the contract is long-term.

Other exempted vehicles are:

    Ambulances, rescue, specialised medical, tractors with enforced speed limit of less than 30 km/h, local agriculture, forestry
    Circus and fun fair
    Specialised breakdown vehicles
    On test for repair or maintenance
    Live animals to and from market, carcasses and raw fish, and animal or food waste unfit for human consumption

Other exemptions are specialised vehicles used for:

Local markets
Door-to-door selling where driver spends large amount of his
    time selling
Mobile banking
Worship
Library
Mobile exhibitions
Transport of milk – farm to depots

SECTION II – INTERNATIONAL

Rules applying to drivers on international journeys including parts
of the journey carried out in the UK.

DRIVERS TO WHOM THIS SECTION APPLIES

Except for the exemptions shown, International rules apply to
drivers of all laden and unladen goods vehicles above 3.5 tonnes
authorised maximum weight, if the driver, or the vehicle, or its
trailer, is leaving or coming to Great Britain.

The AETR is an agreement which embodies countries which are
not members of the EEC, and when hauling outside the EEC the
AETR agreement applies.

AETR countries are: Austria, Czechoslovakia, East Germany,
Norway, Portugal, Soviet Union, Spain, Sweden, Yugoslavia.

Basically, AETR rules require the same as EEC rules but
currently there are five differences:

(a) Daily rest cannot be split into two to allow for ferry or train
    journeys.
(b) Tachographs are not provided for and control books are
    used. Distance limits still apply if tachograph used.
(c) Regular service operators must still use individual control
    books.
(d) If a journey needs to be completed or broken then con-
    tinuous driving can be increased from four to 4½ hours.
(e) The weekly rest period is 24 hours instead of 29 hours.

These differences apply only when you are operating in the
countries mentioned above, and the rules (a) to (e) are in addition
to the following regulations in this Section which are the EEC
agreement rules.

BASIC HOURS LIMITS

Daily driving   8 hours

Although an increase on the weekly driving limit is not allowed, the daily driving limit can be increased twice a week to nine hours. This, however, does not apply to artic combinations of over 20 tonnes maximum weight.

Daily duty   11 hours

Daily spreadover   12½ hours

Daily rest   11 hours

When at work a driver must have had 11 hours rest during the past 24 hours. This can be taken on the vehicle but only if a bunk is fitted and the vehicle is stationary.

If the driver is compensated the 11 hours can be cut to nine twice a week if the rest is taken at base. If away from base the 11 hours can be cut to eight hours, or to one of each of eight and nine hours.

Vehicles which have two drivers and a bunk: A driver, each time he is on duty, must have eight hours continuous rest in the past 30 hours. If the vehicle has no bunk it is 10 hours in the last 27 hours.

The rest period can be split into two, but only in circumstances which include a ferry crossing, and a bunk has to be available during both parts of the rest period.When one part is taken on the ferry the second part must be increased by two hours, and these must be taken immediately before or after joining or leaving the ferry.

Weekly driving   48 hours

Fortnightly driving   92 hours

Bear in mind again that this rolling week is any period of seven consecutive days. At any time a driver is on duty, to calculate hours, he must look back over the previous 168 hours, from that time. The same applies to fortnightly, or the past consecutive 14 days.

Weekly duty   60 hours

Weekly rest   29 hours

This period must be taken in one uninterrupted break immediately before or after a daily rest period. If required, five hours of weekly rest period can be taken off with any daily rest period in the same week.
Remember: A week is any period of seven consecutive days.

Continuous driving   4 hours

Continuous duty   5½ hours

Bonus payments

These payments, where they affect miles or the amount of load carried, cannot be paid where to do so would endanger road safety.

Breaks

The continuous driving limit can be anticipated and this ½ hour break may be split into two 20-minute breaks or three 15-minute breaks, which must be spaced out over and immediately follow the maximum of four hours continuous driving. However, drivers of (a) a motor vehicle or tractor with one semi-trailer in excess of a maximum of 20 tonnes, or (b) a motor vehicle or tractor with more than one trailer or semi-trailer, must take one hour break, but this can be split into two ½-hours. But again ensure that, if the break is split, the continuous driving limit is not exceeded.

Mileage limits

These are the same requirements as in Section I.
Remember: The continuous driving period cannot be extended but *in emergencies* the distance limit, the daily hours limit, the weekly driving hours limit and the daily rest requirements can be broken in the following circumstances:

(a) In case of danger, or in circumstances beyond the driver's control.

(b) To render assistance, as a result of breakdown, to the extent necessary to ensure the safety of persons or the load of the vehicle.

(c) To enable the driver to reach a safe stopping place or, depending on circumstances, the end of his journey.

Emergencies

The continuous driving period cannot be extended, but in emergencies the periods as set out under Emergencies in Section I are applicable.

Special needs exemptions

Where limits can be extended are set out in an Appendix to this Chapter.

Exemptions

Exemptions from this Section

If these apply then refer to Section III.

Vehicles exempted are those used by:
  Civil Defence
  Drainage and flood prevention authorities
  Water, gas, electricity services
  Post Office (mail carriage)
  Telephone services
  Highway authorities
  Refuse collection
  Radio, television and detection vans
  Other public-authority vehicles used for public services
provided that none of the above is in competition with professional road hauliers.

Note: Vehicles on contract from private firms to exempted authorities are not exempt from this Section unless the contract is long-term.

Other exempted vehicles are:
  Ambulances, rescue, specialised medical, tractors with enforced speed limit of less than 30 km/h

Local agriculture, forestry
Circus and funfair
Specialised breakdown vehicles

SECTION III – DOMESTIC

These rules also apply to vehicles on an international journey in the UK where it is a vehicle exempted from Section II.

Basically this section applies to all drivers who are exempted from Sections I and II, i.e. the drivers of vehicles of up to 3.5 tonnes maximum weight and all vehicles in the exemption parts of these Sections mentioned.

But refer to Special Needs Exemptions at the end of this Chapter.

BASIC HOURS LIMITS

Daily driving   10 hours

Note: If some driving is done off the highway, for example in quarrying, agriculture, forestry or building work, then this time does not count in the 10-hour driving limit but it does count as duty time.

Important: Milk transporters operating between farm and depot have a special maximum driving limit of 108 hours in a fortnight and a limit of five hours continuous driving at any one time. This is subject to review, possibly in 1982.

Daily duty   11 hours

Daily spreadover   12½ hours

Important: In this Section a 'week' is fixed as the period between midnight any Saturday until midnight the following Saturday. Variations on this can be obtained on application from local Department of Transport offices.

The 11 hours limit daily duty can be spread over to 12½ hours, if the excess is taken off duty.

If a driver does not drive for more than four hours each day of the week, he is exempted from daily duty, daily spreadover and weekly duty limits for that week. He is also exempt from daily duty limits when he is at work but does not drive.

Weekly duty   60 hours

Continuous duty   5½ hours

Breaks   ½ hour

A driver must take a ½-hour break when he has been on duty for 5½ hours. He is exempt from this part if he is on duty but does not drive, or if he does not drive more than four hours on each day of the week.

Daily rest   11 hours

Special cases

Where this limit can be extended will be found as an Appendix to this Chapter. Generally there must be 11 hours rest between two separate days duty.

Weekly rest   24 hours

This must be taken as a continuous 24 hours, but it can commence in one week and end in the next. But if this is the case it cannot be counted as weekly rest for the purposes of the second week.

The above can be reduced under the heading of Special Cases in the Appendix to this Chapter.

There are also special arrangements where there is danger to life or health in cases of serious occurrences with gas, water, electricity, sewers, postal services, telephones, roads, airports and damage to property.

Exemptions

Exemptions from this Section

Goods vehicles and dual-purpose vehicles inder 3.5 tonnes authorised maximum weight used by:

Veterinary surgeons
Doctors
Nurses, midwives
Dentists
Commercial travellers
AA, RAC, RSAC
Radio, television, cinematograph
Vehicles used for any service, inspection, cleaning, repair, fitting, etc.

Note: None of the above can exceed the daily driving of 10 hours.

SECTION IV – MIXED DRIVING

This Section applies in some cases to drivers who work under more than one Section in any period of a 'week'.

DRIVERS MIXING SECTION I (NATIONAL) WITH SECTION III (DOMESTIC)

Note: (a) If you stick to the limits under section I you will keep within the law under Section III as well.
   (b) When driving under Section III observe the following limits and read each note.
   (c) Make sure, when adding both types of hours together, that the prescribed limits are note exceeded.

BASIC HOURS LIMITS

Daily driving   10 hours

The total amount of driving must be counted from all different vehicles driven and is the same limit as permitted by Section III, but vehicles which come under Section I must still keep within their limits.

Daily duty   11 hours

Daily spreadover   12½ hours

A driver whose duty is spread over 12½ hours must spend the excess off duty.

The four hours a day concession applies, and if he works no longer on each day of the week, he is exempt from daily duty, weekly duty and daily spreadover for that week, which also applies if he is at work but does not drive.

However, on non-driving days the first 11 hours off duty still count on the weekly duty total.

Vehicles double-crewed can extend the spreadover in certain circumstances, as given in the notes below under Daily Rest.

Special cases

Where daily and weekly limits can be extended will be found as an Appendix to this Chapter.

Weekly duty   60 hours

A 'week' is, in this Section, any period of seven consecutive days, and the 'rolling week' applies. This means that for the purposes of limits a driver must look back over the last 168 hours to determine his present position.

Again the same applies to a fortnight period.

Continuous driving   4 hours

Applies only when driving Section I vehicles.

Continuous duty   5½ hours

Breaks   ½ hour

A ½-hour break must be taken after 5½ hours on duty, but drivers of either (a) motor vehicles and tractors with more than one trailer or semi-trailer and in excess of 20 tonnes, or (b) motor vehicles or tractors with more than one trailer or semi-trailer, can split the break into two periods of 20 minutes or three periods of 15 minutes, spread over and immediately following the continuous duty period limit.

Daily rest   11 hours

Drivers must have 11 hours rest between two working days, but again there are certain relaxations to this rule. They are:

   (a) For double-crewed vehicles which have a bunk, the 11 hours can be reduced to eight hours during the preceding 30 hours on duty, that gives a 22-hour spreadover.
        If this type of vehicle is used but has no bunk each driver must have at least 10 hours during the preceding 27 hours on duty, that gives a 17-hour spreadover.
   (b) Twice a week 11 hours rest can be reduced to two periods of nine hours where the rest is taken at base. This can be reduced to two periods of eight hours where the driver is away from base, or to one of each of eight and nine hours.

Weekly rest   29 hours

The weekly rest must be taken in one stretch immediately before or after a daily rest period.

SPECIAL NOTES

DRIVERS MIXING SECTION I (NATIONAL) WITH SECTION II (INTERNATIONAL)

If a driver has done International (Section II) driving at the start of any rolling week then he must carry on with Section II limits all the time.

DRIVERS MIXING SECTION II (INTERNATIONAL) WITH SECTION III (DOMESTIC)

If a driver under this heading sticks to the rules of Section II, he will keep within the law.

He can extend his driving time to 10 hours at any time during the rolling week, which is the Section III limit, but he must not exceed eight hours if the vehicle he is driving is a Section II vehicle.

Under this mixture the weekly rest is 24 hours and this must be taken in one stretch. If, however, this rest falls in a substantial period of Section II work, an extra five hours must be added to the 24 hours or taken with daily rest periods at some other time in the rolling week to which that rest period relates.

Continuous driving   4 hours

Breaks

If a driver under Section II drives for four hours he must take a one-hour break, that's if the vehicle is either (a) a motor vehicle or tractor with one trailer or semi-trailer and in excess of 20 tonnes total maximum, or (b) a motor vehicle or tractor with more than one trailer or semi-trailer.

This break can be split into two ½-hour breaks, but ensure that the continuous driving limit is not exceeded.

Other Section II drivers on continuous driving limit must take a ½-hour break, but this can be split into two 20-minute breaks or three 15-minute periods, spread over and immediately following the four-hour driving limit.

A driver of a Section III vehicle must have a ½-hour break after 5½ hours, but if it is an artic over 20 tonnes maximum, this can be split into two 20-minute periods or three 15-minute periods spread over and immediately following the 5½ hours.

DRIVERS MIXING SECTION I (NATIONAL), SECTION II (INTERNATIONAL) AND SECTION III (DOMESTIC)

Basically the same rules apply as are set out under the previous heading of Drivers Mixing under Section II (International) and Section III (Domestic).

GENERAL NOTES

Private driving

Remember: The EEC regulations do not provide for private driving as an exemption.

If the vehicle you are driving is a goods vehicle under the Regulations, whenever you are driving it, you are well advised to comply with the hours limits. This applies even if you are using the vehicle in a 'private' capacity in connection with, say, a hobby, unless it is a vehicle that comes entirely within Section III (Domestic) rules.

Offences

Hours offences do not carry a licence endorsement, but licensing authorities take these into account when renewing operators' licences or HGV licences.

An employer is protected if a driver commits an offence doing other driving jobs which the employer has no knowledge of or could not have reasonably known about.

Note: This applies to any Section.

Table of Hours Limits

ONE OR MORE SECTIONS APPLY TO DRIVERS OF ALL GOODS VEHICLES CONSTRUCTED OR ADAPTED TO CARRY OR HAUL GOODS. FOR VEHICLES MANNED BY SECOND DRIVERS, SEE TEXT.

	Section I	*Section II*	*Section III*	*Section IV*
Daily driving	8	8	10	10
Daily duty	11	11	11	11
Daily spreadover	12½	12½	12½	12½
Daily rest	11	11	11	11
Weekly driving	48	48	*N/A	*N/A
Fortnightly driving	92	92	*N/A	*N/A
Weekly duty	60	60	60	*N/A
Weekly rest	29	29	*24	29
Continuous driving	4	4	* 5½	* 5½
Continuous duty	5½	5½	5½	5½
Breaks	½	½	½	½
Mileage limits	**450km a day		*N/A	*N/A
Emergencies	no limit, only on continuous driving: 4		no limit, only on continuous driving: 5½	
Special cases	as listed in the Appendix following			
Bonus payments	must not pay		N/A	N/A
Exemptions – see pages 70–71	74–75		76	N/A

Notes relating to Table of Hours Limits:

*In Sections III and IV it will be seen that limits are either not applicable (N/A) or hours differ from Sections I and II. Examples of this are to be found under the headings of:

Weekly driving	Continuous driving
Fortnightly driving	Emergencies
Weekly duty (Sec. IV)	Bonus payments
Weekly rest (Sec. III)	Exemptions

Sections III and IV have no weekly or fortnightly limits because the driver is given the benefit of the Transport Act and not EEC rules. However, he is reminded not to exceed the limits laid down under each Section.

In Section III the difference in weekly rest of 24 instead of 29 is again because this Section is pure Transport Act requirements, therefore EEC limits do not apply.

Continuous driving limits in Sections III and IV will depend upon what sort of driving is being done. If the driver is driving a vehicle purely on national work he must not exceed four hours *continuous driving*. If he is driving purely domestic he can take 5½ hours *continuous duty* which can be made up of either *all driving* or *duty and driving*.

**450km (280 miles) a day: unless vehicle has second driver or is on tachograph.

Milk transportation hours limits: in Section III, these are subject to review. At present they are:

Maximum driving fortnightly: 108 hours   Continuous driving: 5 hours

Duty: is defined as driving combined with other work.

Driving: is defined as time spent at the wheel.

APPENDIX

SPECIAL CASES

Relaxation in hours enabling drivers to deal with emergencies and special operations

These are additional to the relaxations mentioned in Sections I and II (National and International).

Section III (Domestic) drivers rules are as set out.

Section I (National), Section II (International), Section IV (Mixed), can benefit from the relaxations, *but* only to a limited extent.

They cannot extend daily driving limits in Section I or Section II (National and International) while driving vehicles subject to those Sections.

They cannot hold up or lay off weekly rest periods while driving Section I or Section II vehicles (National and International).

They cannot extend daily duty or spreadover where it would conflict with daily rest periods as required by Section I or Section II vehicles (National and International).

SPECIAL NEEDS EXEMPTIONS

The numbers alongside these definitions correspond with the numbers in Column 1 of the scales on pages 84 to 87.

(1) An occurrence required to prevent danger to life or health. Serious, gas, water, electricity and drainage emergencies, and those connected with telephones, postal services, the use of roads or airports, and damage to property.

(2) Work wholly or partly in handling Christmas and New Year mail.

(3) Work wholly or partly done in carriage of food and drink: on Bank Holidays or in the Christmas, New Year, Easter, May, Spring and 'Summer holiday' periods.

The exact periods to which (3), (4), (5) and (6) apply are:

(i) The working week in which Good Friday falls.

(ii) The working week immediately preceding May Bank Holiday.

(iii) The working week immediately preceding that in which the Spring Bank Holiday falls.

(iv) The six working weeks immediately preceding the working week in which the Summer Bank Holiday falls.

(v) The working week in which 1 January falls and the two immediately preceding working weeks.

(4) Work wholly or mainly in carriage of bread.

(5) Work wholly or mainly in carriage of milk.

(6) Work wholly or mainly in carriage of liquid egg in bulk.

(7) Work wholly or mainly in carriage of animals.

(8) Work wholly or mainly in carriage of animal waste not fit for human consumption.

(9) Work wholly or mainly in removal of raw fish. Agricultural produce during harvest. Agricultural lime, seeds, fertilisers, animal feed. Recently-felled trees. Repairing of harvesting machines or delivery of fuel for such machines.

(10) Blood transfusion delivery.

(11) Distribution of magazines or newspapers.

(12) Carriage of furniture between house and storage places.

(13) An abnormal load which owing to its size is escorted by Police for all or most of its journey.

(14) By sea within Great Britain.

(15) Carriage of shop fittings to or from shops.

(16) Carriage of explosives.

(17) Carriage of radio-active materials.

(18) Delivery of stores to ships.

(19) Carriage of materials or components to or from building or civil engineering works.

84

		AT THE WHEEL maximum	ON DUTY maximum	SPREADOVER maximum	BREAKS minimum	DAILY REST minimum
1	Emergencies	No	11	No	No	10 If interrupted, 10 in aggregate
		Applies only during emergency				
2	Post Office	10	14	14	½	11
3	Food/drink	10	14	14	½	11
4	Milk	10	14 Either on Friday, on Saturday or on two working days in week preceding a Bank Holiday, or on any working day in the rolling week detailed in Note (3) (11 on other days)	14 (12½ on other days if 1½ spent on duty)	½	11
5	Milk	10	14 On any day in the rolling weeks covered in Note (3) (11 on other days)	14 (12½ on other days if 1½ spent off duty)	½	11
6	Liquid eggs	10	14 On any day in the rolling weeks covered in Note (3) (11 on other days)	14 (12½ on other days if 1½ spent off duty)	½	11
7	Animals	10	14	14	½	10
8	Animal waste	10	14	14	½	10
9	Raw fish, timber, farm goods, farm machinery	10	14	14	½	11

10 Blood transfusion	10	14 (on two days each week and four hours must be taken for rest and refreshment) (11 on other days)	14 (12½ on other days if 1½ spent off duty)	½	11
11 Newspapers, magazines	10	14	14	½	10
12 Furniture removal	10	14	14	½	11
13 Long/wide/heavy loads	10	11	14	½	11
14 Crossings	10	11	14	½	11
15 Shop fittings	10	14	14	½	11
16 Explosives	10	14	14	½	11
17 Radio-active material	10	14	14	½	11
18 Ships' stores	10	14	14	½	11
19 Building/civil engineering	10	14	14	½	11

Note: 'Week' in this Appendix means the same whatever the work being carried out, i.e. in Sections I, II, III, IV

Daily duty under general rules

10	11	12½	½	11

WEEKLY ON/OFF DUTY HOURS

		ON DUTY maximum	OFF DUTY minimum
1	Emergencies	66 Emergency work	24 Each week, taken within four weeks: if last 24 hours period in working week is interrupted, then not required to comply
2	Post Office	66	24 Each week, taken within four weeks
3	Food/drink	66	24 Each week, taken within four weeks
4	Bread	66 (In the working week detailed in Note (3)) 60 (In any other week)	24 Each week, taken within four weeks
5	Milk	66	48 In two weeks
6	Liquid eggs	66	24 Each week, taken within four weeks
7	Animals	66	24 Each week, taken within four weeks
8	Animal waste	66	24 Once each week
9	Raw fish, timber, farm goods, farm machinery	66	24 Each week, taken within four weeks
10	Blood transfusion	60	24 Once each week
11	Newspapers, magazines	60	24 Once each week
12	Furniture removal	60	24 Once each week

13	Long/wide/heavy loads	66	24 Each week, taken within four weeks
14	Crossings	60	24 Once each week
15	Shop fittings	60	24 Once each week
16	Explosives	60	24 Once each week
17	Radio-active material	60	24 Once each week
18	Ships' stores	60	24 Once each week
19	Building/civil engineering	66	24 Each week, taken within four weeks

INDEX